# WORKING WOODEN TOYS

Marion Millett is the author of *Wooden Toys That Work*
and creator of Whim-Wham Toys

# Marion Millett
# WORKING WOODEN TOYS

Illustrated by Michael Hanson
Photography by Paul Bock

BLANDFORD PRESS
POOLE · DORSET

STERLING PUBLISHING CO., INC.
NEW YORK

First published in the UK 1985 by Blandford Press,
Link House, West Street, Poole, Dorset, BH15 1LL

Distributed in the United States by
Sterling Publishing Co., Inc.,
2 Park Avenue, New York, NY 10016

**British Library Cataloguing in Publication Data**

Millett, Marion Cathcart
    Working wooden toys.
    1. Wooden toy making
    I. Title
    745.592            TT174.5.W6

Hardback ISBN 0 7137 1565 0
Paperback ISBN 0 7137 1688 6

Typeset by Colset Pte. Ltd., Singapore
Printed in Great Britain by R.J. Acford Ltd., Chichester, Sussex

In gratitude to Rudolf Steiner
Whose teachings are the inspiration
of my toymaking and of this book

# CONTENTS

# ACKNOWLEDGEMENTS

In the making of this book, a number of people have helped with welcome advice and suggestions. To all of whom I wish to express my thanks. In addition, I am particularly grateful to the following:
— Taco and Ita Bay, Angus Mackinnon and the late Robert Vinestock, whose help and encouragement in toymaking led to the writing of my first book, *Wooden Toys that Work*, and to Ita also for her delightful dwarf design for my Whim-Wham toys.
— Jack Vinestock and grandson Alistair, for general expertise and help in making model drums.
— Duncan MacNeill, who devoted much time and skill to making many of the preliminary drawings, and helped with a number of creative ideas and techniques.
— Peter Barnes, musician and photographer, who made many imaginative studies of my toys in black and white.
— Paul M. and Joan de Ris Allen, whose help was vital in bringing this book to completion.
— R.T. Hutchings, for several years Curator of the Museum of Childhood, Edinburgh, who supplied much information.
— Jack Dinnie, who always knows how things work and how to make them work.
— Michael Hanson, a most skilful and resourceful craftsman, who worked out the way to make the Pecking Bird and Skippy, and who has provided the illustrations.
— Patricia Hunter, who devoted precious free time to typing my manuscript so carefully and well.
— Fred Murray of Murray's Tools, Morrison Street, Edinburgh, who found me a splendid electric jigsaw (Rockwell Scroll saw) second-hand, and who is always ready with good tools and good advice.
— Mrs Hilary Kirkland, Education Officer of Age Concern Scotland, who made my toymaking known to many people through a splendid write-up in *The Scotsman* by her journalist friend, Mrs Janet Rae, and by a wonderful presentation of my toys on Channel 4 television in a film made by her film-director friend, Patricia MacLaurin, and the team of Sidhartha Films.
— Paul Bock, who devoted much care to the difficult task of arranging and photographing toys of so many different shapes and sizes.
— John Newth, Editorial Director of Blandford Press, most courteous and considerate of publishers.
— Finally, my son Duncan, Ingrid his wife, and their children Christopher and Miranda, and my daughter Joanna, all of whom kept me supplied with helpful material from many sources, and whose interest and enthusiasm were indispensable.

## AUTHOR'S PREFACE

When my children were quite young, the educational ideas of Rudolf Steiner, the great Austrian philosopher and educationist, interested me so much that I started a Nursery Class on the lines which he indicated in the Surrey village where we were living. One of Rudolf Steiner's suggestions was that small children should have movable wooden toys, toys to which they could do something that would produce an effect. As it was wartime and good wooden toys no longer came to us from Germany, some of the parents of our little school got together and made some which were quite successful and much appreciated.

As the children grew bigger, and the war came to an end, the school came to an end too, and with it my toymaking, which I did not take up again until forty years later. By this time, I had returned to Scotland to live in Edinburgh, my native city. Some friends needed help with a toystall for a church sale of work, and I began making toys with even greater enthusiasm, fired by kindred spirits and a new incentive. In my new home I was able to turn a tumble-down garden shed into a pleasant little workshop with electricity laid on for power tools.

Over the last fifteen years and somewhat spasmodically, I have made many toys and gradually come to the realization that their movements derive from certain basic principles which can be diagnosed and classified.

By different applications of the underlying movement, quite new toys can be evolved. The results are shown in this book. The most notable example to my mind is the Spanish toy which I have called Men at Work, or Tom, Dick and Harry. It is a delightful and uniquely different toy from the well-known Pecking Hens, but both are motivated in identical fashion.

Some eight or nine of the toys described here, sometimes in changed form, were included in my first book on Toymaking, *Wooden Toys that Work*, which was published by Messrs Mills & Boon Ltd in November 1974, but has been out of print since 1978.

Marion Cathcart Millett,
Edinburgh, 1985

## INTRODUCTION

### The Triumphant Toymaker

The image evoked by the subject of this charming and practical book is dear to the heart of every child and is one which lives in the memory of every adult. For who has not imagined the old-time toymaker as Dickens, for example, has immortalised him in the figure of Caleb Plummer?

*... a little, meagre, thoughtful, dingy-faced man whose absorbed and dreamy manner would have set well on some alchemist, the distraught air of a man who was casting about for the Philosopher's Stone. His wandering and thoughtful eye seemed to be always projecting itself into some other time and place... In the little cracked nutshell of a house where he lived and worked were houses, furnished and unfurnished for Dolls in all stations of life, Noah's Arks in which Birds and Beasts were an uncommonly tight fit, and where it was difficult to distinguish which were Shems and Hams and which were Wives... Tumblers in tight red breeches were incessantly swarming up high obstacles and coming down, head first, on the other side, not to mention beasts of all sorts, horses in particular of every breed, as well as dozens of grotesque figures...*

But this present book is not merely something which can make a real or fancied past live again for the reader, or — we hope — the *doer*, for whom it is primarily intended. It is essentially a book for the present, a book designed to be of practical help to anyone concerned with the need for toys which appeal to the child in a way that much currently being offered does not do. For, in contrast to the synthetic products of a technologically-based world, the child instinctively longs for toys made from natural substances, for such toys can give real satisfaction and lasting enjoyment.

Parents, teachers, craftsmen and many others will welcome this unusual and helpful book. Essentially it is an invitation to activity, to *doing* rather than to a simple perusal of its pages. It is a manual, reminding one of *manus* — the hand — with all the latter's creative possibilities, a manual which calls one to the employment of these possibilities in service of the child.

In the following pages, Marion Millett, Edinburgh-born toymaker and designer of toys, offers the possibility that anyone who simply follows her indications and guidance can become not only a joyful, but — even more wonderful — a TRIUMPHANT toymaker!

By means of her simple, step-by-step directions and patterns (the latter can be traced directly on the wood from the pages of this book), Mrs Millett leads the would-be toymaker to a result satisfying to himself or herself and — unquestionably more important — to the child into whose hands the fruit of his or her work will come.

From the contents page it will be noted that the keynote of the toys presented in this particular book is *movement* of various types. Movement, especially *rhythmic* movement is one of the most fundamental means of expression and communication. In the hands of the gifted painter, musician or poet it can enhance our lives. Therefore, in accentuating movement as a special aspect of the art of toymaking, Mrs Millett has touched upon a vitally important factor in human experience. For movement, properly directed and balanced, can serve as a therapeutic element in preserving much that our contemporary life threatens to destroy.

For many years a close student of the wealth of creative inspiration and practical guidance which Rudolf Steiner has brought to the development of an educational praxis suited to the needs of the growing child, Mrs Millett is well aware of the importance of properly unfolded movement at various stages of the child's life. For example, rocking, rolling, levering, pivoting, springing, swinging, striking all lead and contribute to the experience of balancing, which in turn can climax in *standing*. Thus, the child slowly relates himself to the world of space and time, into which by degrees he penetrates with the instinctive, ultimate aim of finding himself increasingly at home upon the earth. Hence, what is included in this book in the form of examples of toymaking is by no means directed toward pleasure and enjoyment alone.

Above all, it is aimed toward the creation of toys which, in a genuinely therapeutic sense, can help the growing child to experience, imitate and master some of the most fundamental types of movement essential to human life. This is perhaps the most far-reaching contribution this book can offer.

To become a Triumphant Toymaker in the fullest sense must mean that one does not simply reproduce toys long familiar to children in many parts of the world, but that one eventually becomes able to create entirely new toys of one's own design, toys never seen before! Therefore, as examples of this latter aspect of the toymaker's art, Mrs Millett has included in this book more than a dozen examples of original toys of her own creating.

The true toymaker has the dual possibility of bringing to today's children what has been inherited from the magic world of the toymaker's art of the past, and at the same time of creating entirely new and exciting toys to enrich the present and the future. When able to do this — and this book will prove useful in achieving this goal — then he or she will no longer be simply a toymaker, but will have become a TOY-MAKER TRIUMPHANT!

Paul M. Allen
Newton Dee Village,
Bieldside, Aberdeenshire,
Scotland

# PART I
# TOYMAKING

## WOODEN TOYS

Making wooden toys is great fun. It is also much more than that: not only does it involve the maker in a most pleasurable activity in which he has scope to exercise his own ingenuity and develop his skills, but it also provides fascinating toys for his children and for other people's children as well. How delightful for a child to have a toy made for itself, especially if the maker is a loving parent or grandparent.

Since I took up toymaking seriously about fifteen years ago, very many people have recalled having similar toys made for them, generally by 'Dad', when they were children, and they are rejoiced to remember their former playthings and something of their childhood with them. It is very refreshing from time to time to connect with our childhood.

In our brash modern civilisation, children's needs are all too often provided for by mass-produced toys of plastic materials, easily broken, crude and garish. They are a disappointment from beginning to end for they neither feel nor look attractive, nor do they stand up to the wear and tear of constant use. The time has obviously come when more parents should set to and make toys once again; and indeed many of them are doing just this. Many more would like to do so if they knew how to set about it, and it is for them that this book is specially written.

Movable wooden toys have been my great interest, and, in my experience, they have a particular fascination for children, as well as for myself. They are educative and allow scope for a child's imagination and powers of fantasy, which more than ever today need strong nurture in childhood. Apart from knowing how to use a fret-saw, a screw-driver and a few basic tools, no training in woodwork is necessary to make these toys. The patterns reproduced in this book are ready to be traced on to wood, and all that is required for success is patience and accuracy. Skill comes with practice, and practice makes perfection.

Toys can be made to move in many different ways, and, once certain basic principles are understood, they can be applied in a variety of situations to produce a great diversity of toys.

Fundamental movements, as I see them, arise from rolling and rocking, the use of springs, pendulum and pivot, torque or twisting movement, parallel and angled bars, jointing and balance in various ways, and by other miscellaneous methods. Toys which incorporate these principles will be dealt with in this book and will, I hope, enable many people to make them from the descriptions and illustrations given; and also to evolve original variations for themselves, and for the delight of their children. This book does not, of course, pretend in any way to be a comprehensive treatise on movement. It only seeks to point out certain aspects of an inexhaustible subject, which can be developed in very many directions.

May I insist again that a good toy gives scope to a child's imagination. It should be pleasant — beautiful if possible — both to look at and to feel: corners should be rounded off, surfaces smoothed and sometimes waxed; colors should be bright and gay, but not garish. The usual toy bricks of uniform shape, color and size are stultifying to a child and effectively bring him up against a brick wall. On the other hand, unusual shapes, semi-circular, triangular, irregular, fire a child's imagination and allow him to construct models for the future.

Much can be learnt from watching children at play; and modifications and developments to toys can be incorporated accordingly. Children's approval and interest are wonderful incentives to further creation, and nothing gives me greater pleasure than to hear that a child cannot bear to be parted from a toy, and has insisted on taking it to bed with him!

From time to time children have discovered latent possibilities which I had not realised in some of my toys. Blondin, for instance, which was designed to rotate on his two feet, balances just as efficiently on one foot and looks much more exciting, not to say spectacular, with the other foot stuck out either forwards or backwards. This was discovered by children fiddling with his legs, which were not riveted as tightly as I had intended. The result so surprised and delighted me that I devised Petronella, a ballerina, to show off this talent. Petronella, by the way, is the name of a Scottish dance with a pleasant, lilting tune to which I used to enjoy dancing when I was a child. Blondin was also developed into a real circus toy by my grandchildren experimenting with several at a time. They put one stand on top of another, then balanced Blondin on top with another Blondin hooked over the beads on each side of his balancing rod, and spun the whole lot round. A truly impressive balancing act! The Three Balancing Blondins.

# EQUIPMENT

So much has been published recently about tools that it seems hardly necessary to repeat such information in this book. I would only like to emphasize that every one of these toys can be made with hand tools, fret-saws, drills, files, sandpaper and so on, and any solid old table will do as a bench. Machine tools can, of course, do the work more quickly and efficiently, while a machine jig-saw, and a power drill or drills with stands for drilling and for sanding are great adjuncts if much toymaking is contemplated.

A see-through plastic ruler is very useful; another helpful tool is a metal ruler carrying an arm at right-angles (90 degrees) at one side and at 45 degrees on the other, with a small spirit-level, this arm is slotted into a groove and is very easily adjustable. The tool is called a Combination and Mitre Square. A Try-square (set-square), pliers of various kinds, small and medium screw-drivers, a small hammer and a sharp penknife are all essential. It is a good habit to keep a sharply pointed pencil and an eraser in your pocket — and always put them back after use because they love to hide. White and red pencils show up best. You will also need a pencil-sharpener, a compass and adhesive or masking tape about $\frac{1}{4}''$ (6mm) to $\frac{1}{2}''$ (12.5mm) wide for strapping pieces of wood together so that you can drill holes and cut two parts of a toy, such as arms or legs, exactly matching. With this equipment, any of the toys in this book can be made.

Surprisingly little wood is required for most of these toys, and all of them can be made out of plywood, which is strong and can be obtained in varying thicknesses. The thickness required will be given with each toy but mostly it will be $\frac{1}{4}''$ (6mm) or $\frac{1}{8}''$ (3mm). Birch and beech plywood are both very satisfactory, though they have now become expensive and are often difficult to obtain.

Scrap wood is often available from timber merchants at little or no cost. Personally I am a miser where wood is concerned and save every scrap I can. It is surprising how useful odd little pieces of board and dowel can be. A timber-merchant or crafts-and-hobby-shop can save you a lot of time and work if you ask for your big pieces, such as the base of Tapsalteerie or the board for Ziggedy Man, to be cut out to the exact size. Parana pine $\frac{1}{2}''$ (12.5mm) thick is ideal for bases and stands, especially a piece with the lovely red grain in it, but alas! it too has become extremely expensive; plywood or ordinary pine can be used instead.

Dowel rods are needed for many toys. They can be bought by the foot in varying diameters from $\frac{1}{8}''$ (3mm) to $1\frac{1}{4}''$ (31mm). Dowel should be chosen carefully because there is variation within the quoted sizes, but the dowel must fit exactly into your drill hole. Half-round dowel of $\frac{3}{4}''$ (18mm) diameter and $\frac{1}{2}''$ (12.5mm) wood are often useful. Half-inch wood is wood which measures $\frac{1}{2}''$ (12.5mm) by $\frac{1}{2}''$ (12.5mm), i.e. it is square and is sold in lengths as required. It can also be had in other sizes such as $\frac{1}{4}''$ (6mm) square, $\frac{3}{4}''$ (18mm) square and so on.

All these things can be obtained from crafts and hobby, or Do-It-Yourself shops. It is well to keep a supply handy because you will always find a need for them; and like everything else nowadays they cost more every time they come into stock.

# PAINTING

Wooden toys are much improved in my opinion by being painted, and children enjoy them much more too. The colors should be bright, gay and harmonious, but there should not be too much detail in features or in dress.

The choice of paint is important because it must be non-toxic, but manufacturers are not obliged to declare their ingredients. It is as well to enquire from them direct if there is any doubt, because, in my experience, suppliers tend to be somewhat vague on the subject. The British company of Messrs Winsor and Newton assure me that their Cotman Water Colours are all completely non-toxic, and I have always found them most satisfactory. They give a matt effect and need to be varnished when dry, for which polyurethane varnish with matt or satin finish is my choice. Humbrol Colour is also non-poisonous and very satisfactory. It comes in neat little tins in a great variety of colors, and gives a gloss finish, but must not have varnish added.

It is fairly common knowledge that there are three primary colors, yellow, blue and red, but not everybody seems clear about the complementary colors, though they are easy to discover by a simple little experiment. Paint a disc of red color on a piece of white paper and gaze at it intently. After a short time its complementary color — green — will appear circling round it. The green is fugitive and luminous and may not appear at once to everyone. This sometimes requires a little practice and perseverance. The moment when you first perceive it is an exciting one, and you realize you have seen what is known as a physiological color, one created by your eye in response to your concentration on a given color. You can also gaze at your red circle for several seconds and then move your gaze to a piece of white paper, when you may see a whole green circle appear upon it. Your eye has created not only the complementary color but has created it in the form of a disc as well! Similarly, if you gaze at a blue disc, an orange complementary color will appear, and if you gaze at a yellow disc, a violet complementary color will appear.

What is very remarkable is the fact that you are experiencing a trinity in color, for each single primary color produces a complementary color which is composed of two colors. Red produces green, which is a combination of blue and yellow. Blue produces orange, which is a combination of red and yellow, and yellow produces violet which is a combination of blue and red.

The opposite effect will also arise: if you gaze at a violet (blue and red) circle, your eye will create a yellow light around it. If you gaze at a green one (blue and yellow) red will appear, and if you gaze at an orange one (red and yellow) blue will appear. A little such practice will soon reveal to you which colors complement each other and awaken your interest in the fascinating phenomena of color and its infinite variety. These ideas are based on Goethe's Theory of Color.

Of course, there is much variation in the shade of each color and you will soon discover if you did not already know, that red, for instance, varies from a blue-red (crimson), to scarlet, which is an orange-red. You will then take scarlet as the correct red to combine with lemon yellow to give the best orange color. Crimson red combined with ultramarine or cobalt blue gives purple, while prussian blue combined with lemon yellow gives the best green. White will lighten and brighten any other color, while even a tiny quantity of black will darken it. Incidentally, if you want to lighten a color, it is quicker and more economical to add some of the color to be lightened to the white rather than to add white to the color because only a small quantity of a darker color is needed to tint white, while a very great deal of white would be needed to lighten a patch of darker color. Needless to say, paint is very expensive nowadays.

It is interesting to experiment with color mixing, either by dropping a small amount of water color, say lemon yellow, into a jar of water, stirring it up, and then adding a very small quantity of prussian blue and watching how they combine magically to produce green, or by simply mixing small amounts of water color on a plate. In this way, you very quickly learn how one color can affect another, and which colors combine harmoniously together.

Observation of rainbows can teach us a lot (when we have

the good fortune to see one) and we can train ourselves to become more conscious of the infinite variety of greens which Nature displays all round us.

Although it is possible to arrive at most shades of color from a basic set of two yellows (lemon and chrome), two blues (ultramarine or cobalt and prussian), two reds (scarlet and crimson), and white and black, and it is most valuable and enjoyable to experiment with colors in this way. I would, nevertheless, recommend for convenience and for saving time, that, in addition to these eight basic colors, you include in your collection an emerald green, a lilac and burnt umber (brown), and maybe a good orange as well. That makes a dozen tubes of color in all, with which you can create a vast range of colorful toys for your own delight and for that of your children and friends.

The best way to use the tubes of color is to squeeze a small amount of paint on to an old plate, and have a jar or jars of clean water and a paint rag and tissues handy. Take a little water on your brush and mix it into the edge of the paint until you get the consistency you want. Always wash your brushes thoroughly when changing from one color to another, and use clean water (keep changing it) so that the colors never become messy.

Painting on wood is a little different from painting on paper, and it is advisable to practise on scrap wood first. Make your wood really smooth by first damping it, allowing it to dry and then sandpapering it. Do not apply the color too wet, use fine paint-brushes except when there is a large surface to be covered, and you will soon find your way. When the paint is absolutely dry, the work should be given at least one coat of clear varnish with a soft brush. A little wax rubbed in and polished off with a soft rag, will give the work a fine finish and make it smooth and pleasant to handle. Note, however, that you should NOT put varnish over Humbrol paint or it will run and spoil completely.

A few final words about painting: do give pleasing expressions to the faces you paint and do not put in too much detail; the ends of mouths should curve upwards in a slight smile; dots are sufficient for eyes; thin, slightly curved eyebrows can be added and that is enough for a face; hair styles should give a softening and pleasing effect — it is fascinating to decide, with your paint-brush in hand and some special child in mind perhaps, whether to create a curly-headed blonde, a brunette, a red-head or a dark-haired beauty!

## DRILLING

Drilling must be done slowly and at right angles to the work, withdrawing the drill from time to time to blow out the accumulated sawdust which can deflect the drill. If a sloping hole is required, as in Tapsalteerie, the wood must be arranged at the angle required and the drill kept upright. If a large hole is required, start by drilling out a small central hole first, then gradually use larger drills until you arrive at the size of hole you want. In moving from a small drill hole to a larger one, a few turns with a counter-sink bit first will prevent the drill from jumping and damaging the hole. Once the drill has just come through to the under side, it is a good idea to turn the wood and enlarge the hole a little from there, so that the final drilling does not fracture the surrounding wood.

When drilling holes in dowel, or near the edge of a piece of wood which might split, fix the dowel or piece of wood in a clamp. It is essential that the article to be drilled is kept firm, especially if you are using an electric drill which is very powerful and can easily knock small objects out of your hand, giving you a nasty jolt at the same time.

Riveting is required for several of the toys in this book. It is not a difficult process and, with a little practice, one soon becomes expert. The rivets should be made of aluminium, which is a soft metal easily bent over. Small, round-headed $\frac{1}{8}''$ (3mm) aluminium rivets and $\frac{1}{8}''$ (3mm) steel washers have been used for the toys in this book, but flat-headed rivets can be used. The length of rivet will be indicated with each toy.

To fix round-headed rivets, it is helpful to use a quite inexpensive tool called a Rivet Set. It is simply a flat piece of metal, varying from $3\frac{1}{2}''$ (87.5mm) to 5″ (125mm) long and $\frac{1}{2}''$ (12.5mm) thick, with a cup-like depression on top. It is fitted into a clamp. Attach the pieces of wood to be joined by putting a rivet through them, adding a washer; and leaving $\frac{1}{8}''$ (3mm) of the rivet sticking up — if there is more, cut off the excess with pliers. Next, lay the round head of the rivet into the cup-like depression of your Rivet Set, which is fixed in the clamp, and gently tap around the projecting end of the rivet with a hammer so that this soft end is spread over the washer sufficiently to prevent the washer from coming off.

A neater result is obtained if you buy a second Rivet Set and lay the cup-like depression on the second set over the projecting end of the rivet, then give one or two firm taps to the Rivet Set and you will find it has rounded off the rivet very smoothly.

Where movement is required in the part riveted, do not make your riveting too tight.

If a very loose joint is required, use a slightly longer rivet and insert a piece of thin metal between the parts you are joining. To do this, cut out a $\frac{1}{8}''$ (3mm) slot in the metal, which can easily be done with a fret, jig, or hack saw; slip the slot around the rivet before you start to hammer, and withdraw it when you have rounded off the end of the rivet onto its washer.

Be patient! Be exact! Never do things in a hurry! Avoid caricature of any kind. Facial expressions should be friendly and pleasant.

When cutting two similar parts of a toy, such as two arms or two legs, trace your pattern on to one piece of wood, and then strap the wood with adhesive or masking tape to a second piece of wood, similar in size, shape and thickness, and make drill holes when required *before* cutting out.

Prepare the surface of your wood well before painting, by dampening it, letting it dry and then sandpapering it. Sand *with* the grain of the wood. After painting or varnishing small parts of toys with drill holes in them, thread them on to fine knitting needles and suspend them over a bowl or box to dry off.

Use plastic string in bright colors for loose joints wherever possible: it gives extra color and flexibility to your toy and saves using screws and rivets. A little touch of glue on the knots will prevent them from coming undone. Be sure to tie a reef, or square, knot which does not slip instead of a granny knot which does.

Strictly speaking a bit is fixed into a drill to make a hole in wood or metal. In practice, a $\frac{1}{4}''$ (6mm) (or any other diameter) *bit* and a $\frac{1}{4}''$ (6mm) *drill* mean one and the same thing, as you will find in these pages.

Always drill holes when they are required *before* cutting out.

To drill a hole to a given depth, say $\frac{1}{2}''$ (12.5mm), stick a piece of masking tape or wind a rubber band as a marker round the drill bit $\frac{1}{2}''$ (12.5mm) from the tip, and do not drill beyond this mark. If you are using an electric drill on a stand, set it so that the drill cannot go deeper than required.

Use a counter-sink round holes which are to receive screws. Use a counter-sink also before enlarging holes: this prevents damage and gives a fine finish.

In fixing screws, if you forget which way to turn:

turn *right* to *tight*en;
turn *left* to *loo*sen.

**Rocking, Rattling and Rolling Toys** Clockwise from 12 o'clock: *top*: Cradle; *top right*: Roller Rattle; *lower right*: Simple Rattle, unpainted; *front*: Rocking Horse; *lower left*: Simple Rattle; *top left*: Rocking toy; *centre*: Rollalong.

**Noise and Wheeled Toys** Clockwise from 12 o'clock: *top*: Clatterbang; *right*: Dumpty Duck; *front right*: Hector; *front left*: Wig-Wag; *left*: Whim.

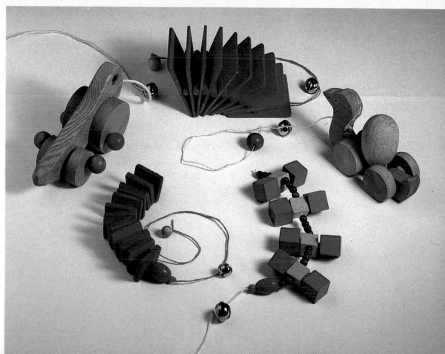

**Rocking and Bent-Axle Toys, and Toys with Springs** Clockwise
from 1 o'clock: *rear right*: Rocking Cow; *right*: Push-Along Chicken;
*front*: Pecking Bird; *left*: Quacking Duck; *rear left*: Jemima; *centre*:
Fluttering Bird.

**Parallel Bar and Twisting Toys** Clockwise from 12 o'clock: *top*: The Brothers; *right*: The Acrobat; *front right*: Twisting-and-Untwisting Toy; *front left*: The Goats; *left*: The Gymnast; *centre*: Ding Dong.

**Jointed Toys** Front row: *left:* Doll; *centre:* The Snake; *right:* Giraffe;
*Rear row:* another Giraffe flanked by two Skippies.

**Balancing, and Gravity and Levity Toys** Clockwise from 1 o'clock:
*top right*: Men-at-Work; *right*: Jingle Bells; *front*: The Magic Waterfall;
*front left and centre*: Two-way Tops; *centre left*: Pussy Cat; *top left*: The
Dwarfs.

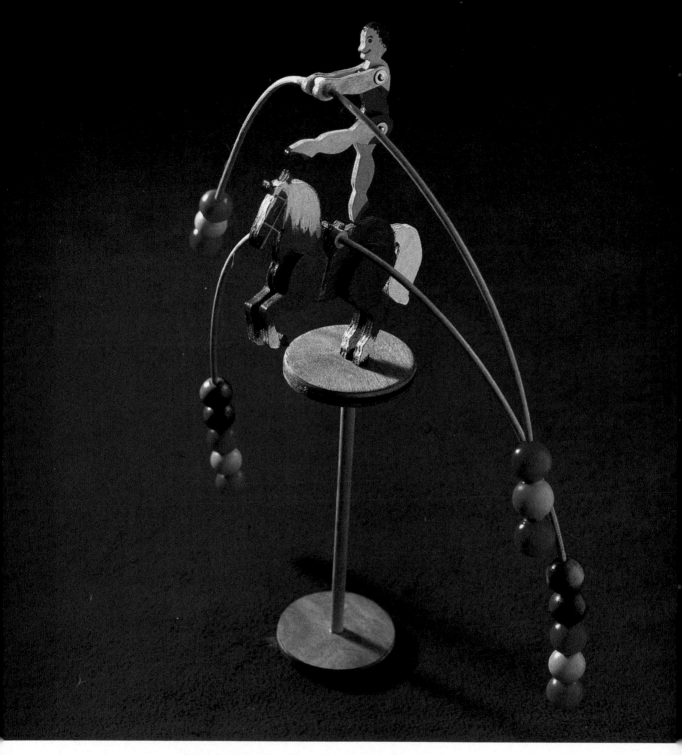

*(Above)* **Balancing Toys** Petronella balancing atop
Pegasus.

*(Above right)* **Balancing Toys** Petronella double-act flanked by
two Blondins.

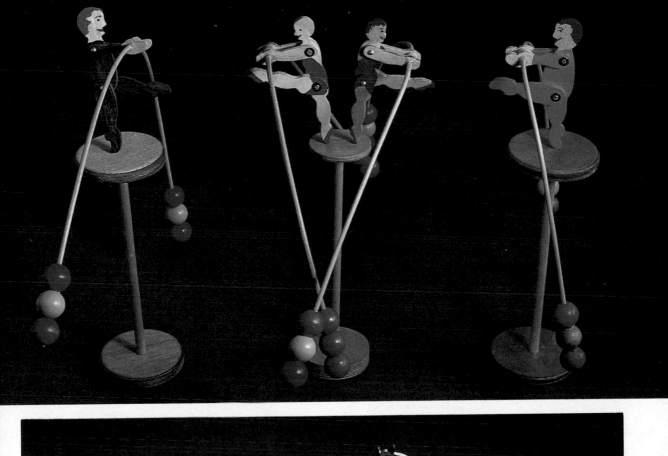

**Balancing, and Gravity and Levity Toys** Clockwise from 1 o'clock:
*right*: Tapsalteerie; *centre right*: The Climber, recumbent; *front*: Spinning
Jack; *left*: Spinning Jenny; *centre*: Ziggedy Man.

# PART II
# FUNDAMENTAL MOVEMENTS

## Rattle, Roller Rattle and Rollalong

One of the first toys given to a baby is a rattle. In earlier days, among the well-to-do, these rattles were often very beautiful, made of silver with an ivory ring or a piece of coral for the baby to chew on to help teething, and with a pleasant jingly bell to distract the baby in times of trouble.

Pleasant little rattles can easily be made in wood. A very simple one consists of three short lengths of dowel with a $\frac{3}{4}$" (18mm) bead, either plain or colored, at either end kept in place by two long pieces of dowel fixed in to opposite corners of little blocks of wood. This is an intriguing toy which baby can shake and finger in absolute safety. It is easy and quick to make.

Rattling can be combined with rolling by putting a big bead loosely on to a short length of $\frac{1}{4}$" (6mm) dowel between two circular pieces of wood. This toy can be rolled along (with baby crawling after it!), or rattled sideways when it makes a gentle knocking noise. An extension of the dowel with a smaller bead fixed on the end makes a convenient hand hold. The roller-rattle illustrated here consists of two discs of 2" (50mm) diameter, cut from $\frac{1}{4}$" (6mm) plywood, which is drilled centrally to take a $\frac{1}{4}$" (6mm) diameter dowel $4\frac{3}{4}$" (118mm) long, and painted in bright colors or simply varnished. One disc is fixed at one end of the dowel, a 1" (25mm) bead with a central hole drilled to $\frac{5}{16}$" (7.5mm) diameter is slipped on, and the second disc is fixed about 2" (50mm) from the first one. (So far we have two fixed discs with a loose bead between them.) Drill another bead centrally to $\frac{1}{4}$" (6mm) diameter this time, and fix it on the other end of the dowel as a handhold, and you have a good toy of the utmost simplicity. Another loose disc between the second one and the end-bead adds to the joyful noise but is by no means necessary. Measurements can vary of course to suit the maker. Be sure to grip the beads in a clamp when drilling.

The very simplest of roller toys can be made by taking a $3\frac{1}{2}$" length of $\frac{3}{4}$" (18mm) wood 2" wide, and drilling a $\frac{5}{16}$" (7.5mm) hole through the width at either end, about 1" (25mm) from the end. Through these holes insert pieces of $\frac{1}{4}$" dowel just over 4" long, and glue large 1" (25mm) colored beads on each end as wheels. This makes a perfect little roll-along toy, right way up or upside down, there is no difference! A child can balance small objects on it, and a hook can be placed at one end if so desired for pulling it along.

These toys are very simple and do not need exact measurements so patterns are not provided. Most of them appear among the toys on the color pages.

# TOYS ON WHEELS

Toys on wheels are very popular with toddlers, and can be produced in infinite variety. Almost any figure can be, and has been, put directly on to wheels: rabbits, horses, ducks and so on — but sometimes the animals are put on a platform with wheels and pulled along.

There are two ways of attaching wheels. They are either attached on to the ends of a loosely rotating axle so that wheels and axle revolve together, or they are attached so that the wheels alone revolve, either by fixing them to the side of a truck or trolley by means of screws or slipping them over a fixed dowel and keeping them in place with a small peg. I much prefer the first method because I do not like screws in children's toys at all. If they are used, they should be counter-sunk to prevent any possibility of scratching. Pegs, too, are unsatisfactory because they break easily or become misplaced.

If the trolley to which the wheels are to be attached is more than an inch (25mm) or an inch and a quarter (31mm) wide, it would be difficult to drill such a long hole accurately. So runners or bearers of $\frac{1}{2}$" (12.5mm) wood can be glued underneath the length of each side, and holes drilled in them for the dowel to pass through. Wheels attached in this way run perfectly satisfactorily without washers and are entirely safe for children to play with, but care must be taken to ensure that the axle holes are in perfect alignment.

Wheels can be made by cutting 1" or $1\frac{1}{4}$" (25 or 31mm) dowel into slices $\frac{1}{2}$" (12.5mm) wide and drilling a hole in the center of each slice. A neat effect is had by not drilling the hole right through, but stopping just beyond half way. This presents an even surface on the outside and conceals the movement of the axle. Some old-fashioned cotton-reels (thread spools) sawn in half make good wheels, and so do large wooden beads. Larger wheels can be made by sawing out circles from a sheet of wood, but is rather difficult to keep wheels made in this way absolutely round, and, if a number are required, it would be advisable to have them turned on a lathe to ensure regularity.

Further variations on toys on wheels can be made by putting the axle off-center on either one or both pairs of wheels. This causes a toy to lollop along, and has been used by many toy-makers to produce amusing ducks, rabbits and such-like. Here, of course, the effect is much increased if the position of the axle is not revealed on the outside of the wheel.

A pull-along toy of an abstract nature with large wheels in the front and small ones at the back was devised by the author and called Whim. Both sets of Whim's wheels are off-center and the movement is emphasised by large colored beads on the outside of each wheel near the edge. These beads are placed opposite to each other, but they do not correspond to the axles. The beads act as stabilizers, and the axles, being off-center, have the effect of making the pairs of wheels now near, then far apart, so that the small back wheels seem to be trying to catch up with the front ones, while Whim's head is alternately lifted up and then lowered, letting the front wheels cover it as if he were hiding his face. A large bell on the string to pull him along further enlivens his progress.

## Whim

From a piece of $\frac{3}{4}$" (18mm) wood, cut out the shape on the opposite page. This is Whim's body. Exactly on the circles marked at each end of it, with centers $4\frac{1}{2}$" (112mm) apart, drill two $\frac{5}{16}$" (7.5mm) holes (a little larger than the $\frac{1}{4}$" (6mm) dowel size of the axles to enable them to revolve freely). Drill a tiny hole in the front of the body to take a ring-screw to which a string can be attached.

From wood slightly thinner than the body, cut two wheels 3" (75mm) in diameter for the front, and two wheels 2" (50mm) in diameter for the back. In each of the four wheels, drill a $\frac{1}{4}$" (6mm) diameter hole, $\frac{1}{2}$" (12.5mm) off center and $\frac{1}{2}$" (12.5mm) deep. Do not drill these holes right through. This is for the sake of appearance as well as for disguising the position of the axle. Paint an eye on each side of the head, and varnish the body and wheels.

On the other sides of all the wheels, which will be the outer sides, drill a hole $\frac{1}{4}$" (6mm) in diameter, $\frac{1}{2}$" (12.5mm) away from the edge and $\frac{1}{2}$" deep. These holes are to receive the short pieces of dowel which will carry the stabiliser beads. Take great care to match their positions on each wheel exactly to each other in relation to the axle holes, so that each pair of beads will be opposite to each other when the toy is in motion. Glue four $1\frac{1}{2}$" (37.5mm) long pieces of $\frac{1}{4}$" (6mm) dowel into these outer holes. Put the two 2" (50mm) axles of $\frac{1}{4}$" (6mm) through the axle holes on the body and glue on the wheels, the large ones in front.

Drill two red and two blue 1" (25mm) beads centrally with a $\frac{1}{4}$" drill. Glue the two red beads on to the projecting ends of dowel on the front wheels, and the two blue ones similarly on to the back wheels. The beads should fit close to the wheels with no dowel showing. Cut off any surplus dowel.

Tie a length of string, with a bell attached an inch or two from the head, on to the ring-screw, tie on a bead at the end of the string as a hand-hold and the toy is ready.

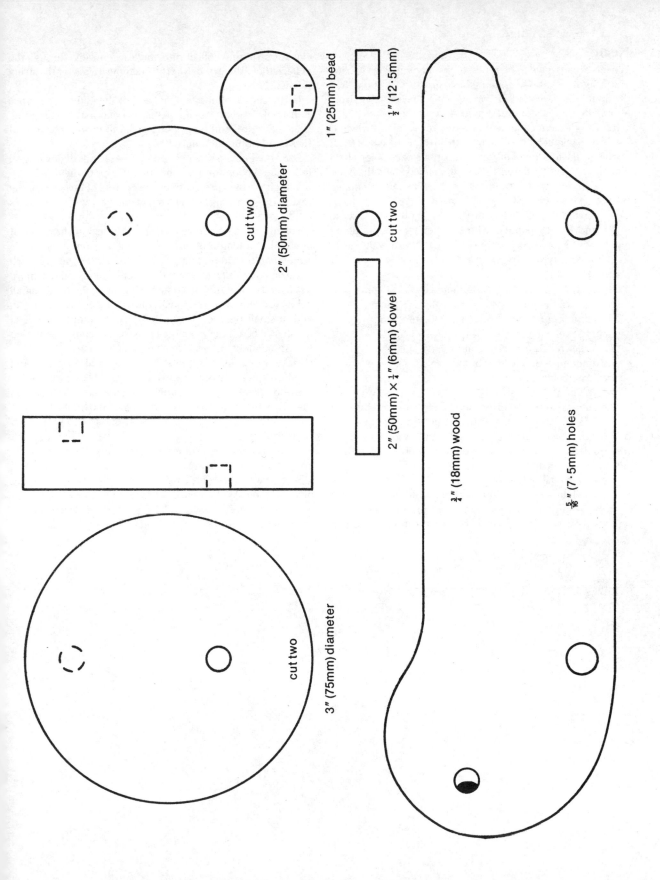

1" (25mm) bead

½" (12·5mm)

2" (50mm) diameter

cut two

cut two

2" (50mm) × ¼" (6mm) dowel

¾" (18mm) wood

5/16" (7·5mm) holes

3" (75mm) diameter

cut two

## Hector

Wheels do not have to be round as was known at least 2,500 years ago! A little wooden horse measuring about $3\frac{1}{2}''$ (87.5mm) high, with four octagonal wheels dating from about 500 B.C. is in a museum in Alexandria.

Recently I have come across a toy from Finland which is motivated in much the same way, in this case, by cubes set at angles to each other. This gives a curious caterpillar effect and makes a gentle clatter as the toy is pulled along the floor. It does this very well if the floor is on a slight slope, but on the level it needs the resistance of a carpet.

My version is called Hector. It is very quick and easy to make and is very popular with small children from about eight months to three years old. It has the advantage of working equally well the right way up or upside down!

Hector needs:

eight cubes 1″ (25mm) by 1″ (25mm) by 1″ (25mm)
four cubes $\frac{3}{4}''$ (18mm) by $\frac{3}{4}''$ (18mm) by $\frac{3}{4}''$ (18mm)
four lengths of $\frac{1}{4}''$ (6mm) dowel $2\frac{1}{4}''$ (56mm) long
twenty-seven small beads [5 + 6 + 6 + 6 + 3 + 1]
two larger beads to indicate neck and head;
one medium bead for handhold;
one large bell;
36″ (900mm) plastic string.

The cubes and the beads should be of wood and brightly colored. Both can be obtained from educational suppliers. It would not be very difficult to make and color one's own cubes if ready-made ones were difficult to obtain. They are certainly not cheap to buy.

And now to make Hector!

Drill the four smaller cubes through the center with a $\frac{9}{32}''$ (7mm) drill, i.e. a little larger than the $\frac{1}{4}''$ (6mm) dowel which is to go through them, to allow for easy rotation, and drill a smaller $\frac{1}{8}''$ (3mm) hole at right angles, centrally, through the cube, either above or below the first hole (this is for the string to pass through).

In the center of one face of each of the eight large cubes drill a hole $\frac{1}{4}''$ (6mm) in diameter, to a depth of $\frac{1}{2}''$ (12.5mm). Glue a $2\frac{1}{4}''$ (56mm) length of $\frac{1}{4}''$ (6mm) dowel into four of these and stand them upright.

Drop the four smaller cubes on to these ends of dowel, and then glue the four larger cubes on the tops of the dowels, so that their corners project over the centers of the sides of the first cubes, forming a star shape. Leave these assemblies until the glue is set.

The toy can now be threaded up. Make a large, firm knot at one end of a length of about three feet (900mm) of plastic string, and thread on five $\frac{3}{8}''$ (9mm) beads for the tail. Push the string through another of the smaller cubes, add six more beads and repeat till you come to the end of the fourth small cube. Add only two beads here, plus a long one for the head, with a small bead on top to look like a minute cap. The number of beads between the cubes can of course be varied to suit the maker's pleasure or his stock in hand.

Make a firm knot in the string to keep all in place, and finally, an inch or two away from the knot, add a large bell to provide a pleasant jingly sound. Add a medium-sized bead at the end of the string for the child to hold, and knot it firmly in place. A touch of glue on all knots is advisable to keep them from coming undone.

Color plays an important part in this toy: the best effects are produced by making all the larger cubes one color, and all the small cubes of a single, contrasting color, selecting beads to tone. As examples, in order of the above, you could use blue, red and green, or yellow, purple and orange, or any other variation you choose.

$2\frac{1}{4}''$ (56mm) $\times \frac{1}{4}''$ (6mm) dowel    cut four

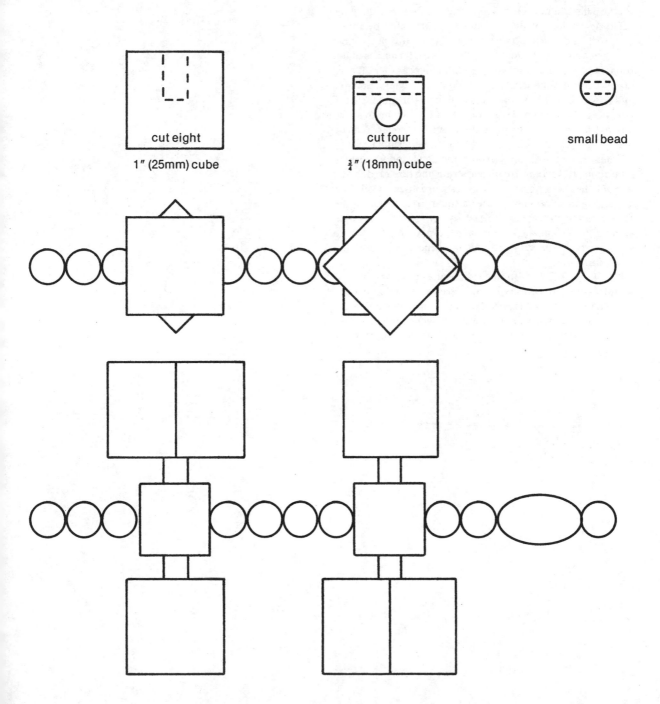

cut eight

1″ (25mm) cube

cut four

$\frac{3}{4}''$ (18mm) cube

small bead

## Clatterbang

Clatterbang is a noise toy, very easy to make, excellent for using up ends of wood, and highly appreciated by three-year-olds. The idea came from a Finnish toy but I have changed and, I think, improved the design. It consists of ten squares of $\frac{1}{8}''$ (3mm) plywood and nine pieces of $\frac{3}{8}''$ (9mm) dowel cut the same length as a side of the square. Squares and dowels are drilled with two small holes on either side of and in a straight line with their centers $1\frac{1}{2}''$ (37.5mm) apart, i.e. each $\frac{3}{4}''$ (18mm) from its center point. The squares can be of any medium size; I find $3\frac{3}{4}''$ (93mm) a very suitable size.

When the squares have been drilled, cut and varnished, take about 4' (1200mm) of plastic string and thread each end through the holes, beginning with a square, then dowel, then a square and so on ending with a square. Tie a knot in the string immediately after the last square, and tie in a bell, about 5" (125mm) higher. Finish the ends of the double strings with a bead as hand-hold, and there is Clatterbang ready for action.

It looks a little like an accordion and makes a pleasant sound as it is moved about, and also a satisfying clatter, tinkle and wiggle as it is pulled along a carpet — it needs the resistance of a carpet or short grass to work properly.

This toy looks especially attractive if it is coated with red or blue varnish.

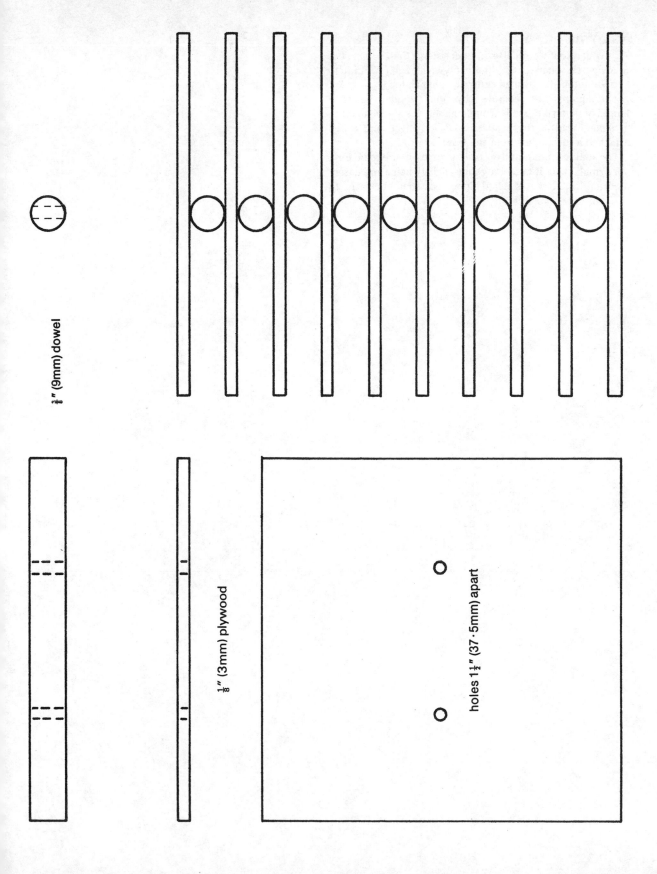

$\frac{3}{8}$" (9mm) dowel

$\frac{1}{8}$" (3mm) plywood

holes 1$\frac{1}{2}$" (37·5mm) apart

## Wig-Wag

Wig-Wag is really a small brother or sister of Clatterbang. It is made of ten squares of $\frac{1}{4}''$ (6mm) plywood, $1\frac{1}{2}''$ (37.5mm) to $2''$ (50mm) in size, drilled centrally and painted.

The squares are separated by small wooden beads: a length of string is passed through the squares and beads with a bigger bead at the head and tail for effect, and a bell attached a few inches from the head.

This makes a delightful pull-along, or toy-in-the-hand for a very small child. It makes a gentle clickety noise and has an amusing wiggle as it is pulled along. It could not be easier to make or more effective.

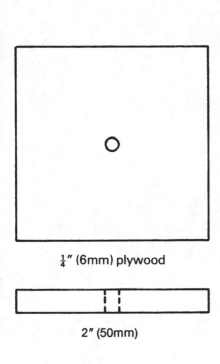

¼″ (6mm) plywood

2″ (50mm)

small bead

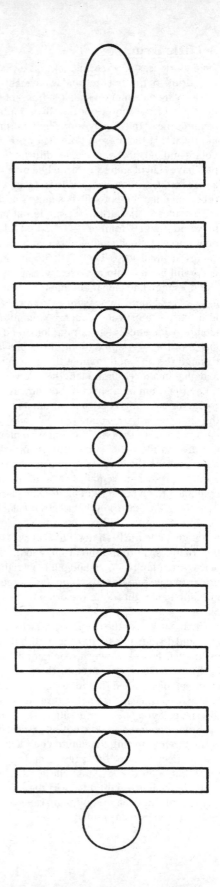

## A Little Drum

On a glorious, sunny, spring day some years ago, I saw this little drum for the first time and was instantly fascinated by it. It was lying on a market stall in a fragrant eucalyptus grove near one of the sources of the River Jordan, and it always reminds me of that lovely spot. Similar drums are being sold in England at the present time. They are very appealing to young and old alike and are not difficult to make. The originals have skin of some sort stretched over them which gives a nice resonant tone, but as skin is not easy to obtain, I have substituted parchment which is quite satisfactory.

The sides of the drum are made out of very fine 3-ply plywood $\frac{1}{32}''$ (0.07mm) or $\frac{1}{16}''$ (1.5mm) thick, which can be bent into a circle. It can be obtained from model shops and comes in small strips $12\frac{1}{2}''$ (312.5mm) wide. Cut a strip $3''$ deep and bend it into a circle, overlapping the ends about $1\frac{1}{2}''$ (37.5mm) and glue them together. Drill a $\frac{1}{4}''$ (6mm) hole — or $\frac{1}{2}''$ (12.5mm), if you want a stronger handle — centrally in a flat piece of wood about $\frac{1}{4}''$ (6mm) or more thick $1''$ (25mm) wide and $2\frac{1}{2}''$ (62.5mm) long, and glue it on to the inside of the overlapping join of the plywood. Drill a hole through the plywood to meet the hole in the strip of wood and glue in a $6''$ (150mm) length of dowel.

Lay the drum on a sheet of parchment and draw a circle round the circumference of the drum on to the parchment — the diameter will be around $3\frac{1}{2}''$ (87.5mm) — and then mark an outer circle of about $1''$ (25mm) greater radius round it. Cut around the outer circle, and then make cuts from the outer circle to the inner as shown in the drawing. Fold back the triangles which remain flat on to the inner circle, then straighten them out at right angles and place the parchment over the drum, ensuring that the triangular pieces fit neatly. Dampen the inner circle with a brush or cloth, but do not let water get on to the triangles. Put a layer of glue, the depth of the triangles, all round the drum, and fix the parchment in place, smoothing it down and pulling it tight — some people prefer to glue one side at a time. Pull some strong, colored, masking tape right round the drum to keep the triangles in place.

When one end of the drum is satisfactorily covered, turn it over and do the same to the other end, but, before doing this, make small holes half-way up each side of the drum, opposite each other, and pass through them a length, about $10''$ (250mm), of stranded thread or very fine string, leaving the ends loose. You can also put in three or four coffee beans at this stage, if you like their additional shuffling sound. When the drum is covered top and bottom, attach beads to the ends of the threads, testing the length you require to get the best sound effects, before tying them on. It is also advisable to make knots on the threads where they emerge from the drum. No skill is required to twirl this effective little instrument around and make sounds guaranteed to drive listeners to distraction in record time!

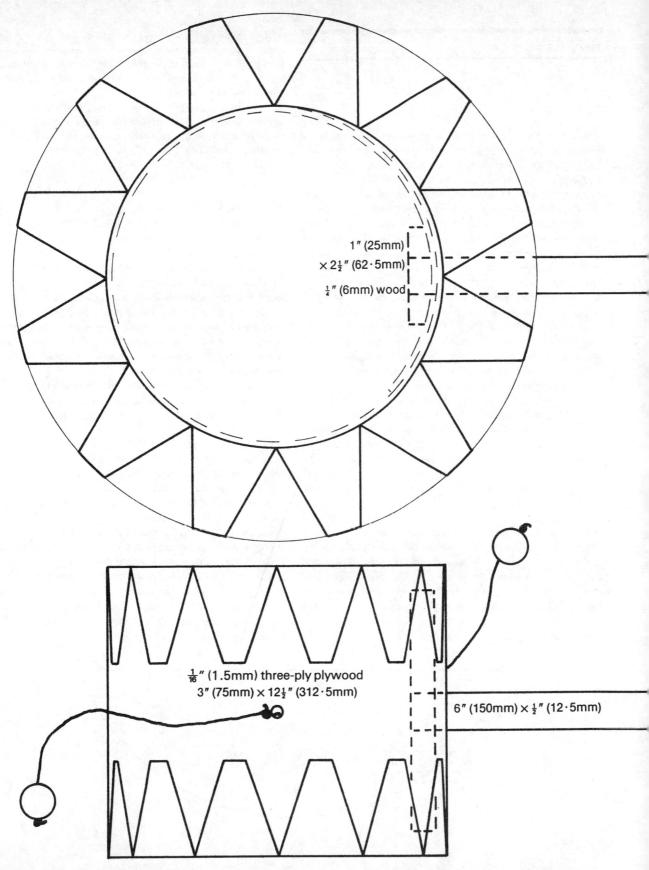

1" (25mm)
× 2½" (62·5mm)
¼" (6mm) wood

1/16" (1.5mm) three-ply plywood
3" (75mm) × 12½" (312·5mm)

6" (150mm) × ½" (12·5mm)

# ROCKING

The simplest form of rocking toy consists of a piece of wood shaped like the arc of a circle, $\frac{1}{2}$" (12.5mm) to $\frac{3}{4}$" (18mm) thick and about $4\frac{1}{2}$" (112.5mm) long on top. This easily shaped piece of wood is the beginning of a highly satisfactory moving toy which will rock, twiddle around, and even turn upside down according to the way it is handled.

The shape suggests a boat, which can easily be developed by drilling vertical holes at either end and inserting 'sailors' made of pipe-cleaners and beads. They are made by doubling a pipe cleaner and drawing the ends through a small, plain, wooden $\frac{1}{2}$" (12.5mm) bead for the head, leaving a piece bent over and glued over the top of the head to hold it in place to look like a cap. The ends of the pipe-cleaner are then put through a larger $\frac{3}{4}$" (18mm) colored bead for the body, leaving the legs to dangle. A piece of cane or dowel is glued into the larger bead from the bottom; it should be long enough to secure the 'sailor' with one end, and to be inserted into the hole in the boat at the other.

This is also a perfectly good toy, and will amuse a small child for considerable lengths of time. It could have a sailor at one end and a bell at the other. A central hole might be drilled to take a mast, to which a stiff paper sail can easily be added. For a small child it is best perhaps to glue in the mast and sailors, but an older child will enjoy changing their positions. Of course, the 'sailors' will often get lost, but they are not hard to replace.

This toy may have the drawback that it tends to tip over when it is being spun round with any force. This is easily overcome by drilling a hole horizontally through the center of the base and putting through it a length of thin dowel, and then glueing small colored beads over the projecting ends of the dowel so that the beads are just level with the bottom of the boat. These beads act as stabilisers and prevent the toy from being easily overturned: they also add a little color. What could be simpler?

The one thing this toy will not do, of course, is sail in water because it will promptly turn over on its side. If a boat is wanted that will sail in the bath, any flat piece of wood will do and it can be shaped roughly fore and aft for realism, and a hole drilled for a mast.

The curved piece of wood occurs frequently in folk toys in various sizes and thicknesses, often with a horse's head glued on at one end, a rider placed centrally, and a wooden or other form of tail attached to the other end — a small rocking-horse in fact.

## Rocking Cow

A very clever use of a similar piece of arc-shaped wood was made by a Boer War prisoner in a toy which is now in the Museum of Childhood in Edinburgh. On the rocker is mounted a piece of wood shaped like the front part of a cow. The head is attached loosely in front and the tail is attached loosely at the back with washers in between. When the toy is rocked, the head and tail swing in a most diverting manner. The original toy, which was probably made with a penknife as the only tool, is skilfully contrived. The drawings given are similar to the original version, but any other breed could well be substituted.

Recently, a toy was in circulation which was no more than an arc of a circle in $\frac{3}{4}$" (18mm) wood with a few indentations on top to look like a hedgehog. A hole was drilled for the eyes.

Instead of using a solid piece of wood, rocking is often brought about by connecting together two pieces of curved thin wood, and mounting a horse or some other animal on top. Rocking chairs and cradles can be made either in this way or with solid rockers. A well-known folk toy rocking-horse of this type is mass-produced in Central Europe nowadays, and exported, charmingly painted and cheaply priced. It rocks very nicely and is quite simple to make. Children enjoy putting a rider on it, and it is easy to provide one by making a little doll out of pipe-cleaners. These little dolls are so simple to make and so useful to children to combine with their other toys that I have included directions for making them under the heading 'Miscellaneous' at the end of the book.

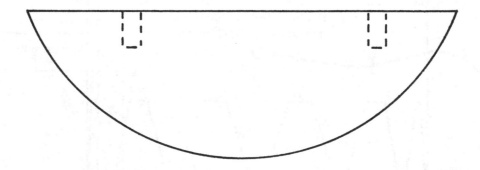

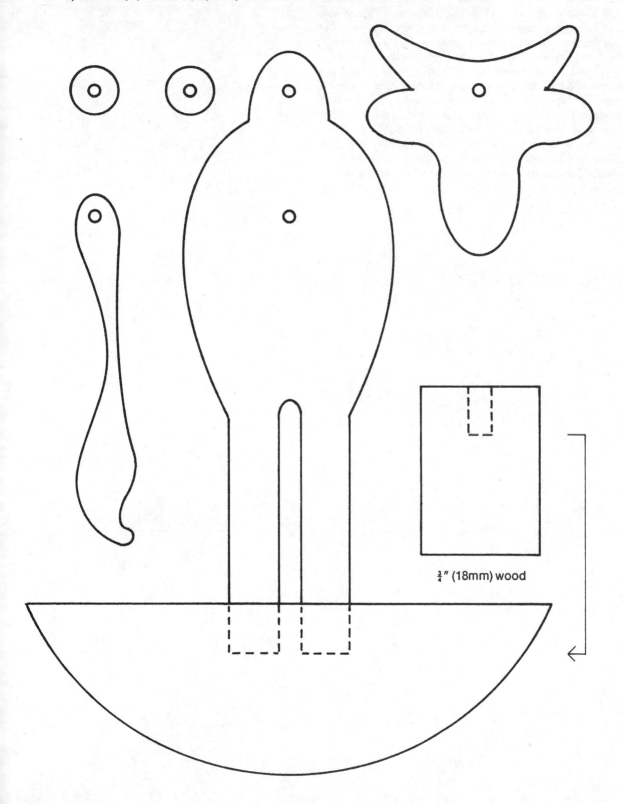

$\frac{1}{4}''$ (6mm) plywood   $\frac{1}{8}''$ (3mm) holes

$\frac{3}{4}''$ (18mm) wood

## Cradle

The cradle is another quick and easy-to-make rocking toy. It can be made of either $\frac{1}{8}''$ (3mm) or $\frac{1}{4}''$ (6mm) plywood. Cut out the top and bottom ends together so that they are identical, and similarly, cut out the two sides together. Cut out the base, and, if you choose, two little strips to strengthen the frame and for support in gluing together, but these are not essential. Glue the base on to one end — call it the top — and, when it is firm, glue the sides on to it, letting them overlap the base slightly for convenience in attaching. When attached, add the bottom end. If it is rocking nicely, as it should be, the cradle can be gently pressed together in a clamp. The cradle is greatly improved by painting, which can most easily be done before the components are stuck together.

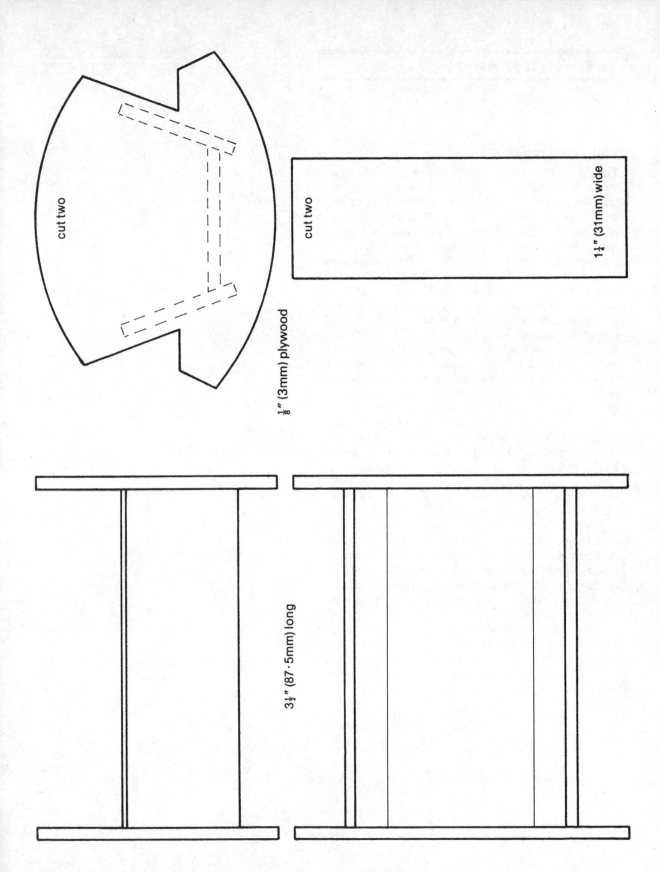

cut two

$\frac{1}{8}$" (3mm) plywood

cut two

$1\frac{1}{4}$" (31mm) wide

$3\frac{1}{2}$" (87·5mm) long

# TOYS WITH SPRINGS

## Fluttering Bird

This little bird which flutters down a wire appears in various forms in various places. One of the simplest and most charming versions which I have found was in Majorca, and it could be of Spanish origin. The toy is very easy and quick to make and gives endless pleasure to child and grown-up alike, though it is too fragile to be given to a small child.

The materials required are minimal. Cut out the head and body as shown in $\frac{1}{4}$" (6mm) plywood. Drill a small hole in the front of the body, $\frac{1}{4}$" (6mm) deep. Glue the head and body together with the beak projecting. Cut out the two wings in $\frac{1}{8}$" (3mm) plywood i.e. thinner than the body. Paint the wings black or green on both sides, and the back of the body and the head black or green. The rest of the bird is white, except the beak and under tail part, which are scarlet and the eye, which is black. When the paint is dry, glue the wings on to the body. Finish the bird by painting small streaks of bright colours here and there, and then varnish it.

Make a stand about 2" (50mm) square from $\frac{3}{4}$" (18mm) thick wood. Drill a hole through the exact center to take a steel rod about $\frac{1}{16}$" (1.5mm) thick and about 12" (300mm) long, held firmly in place with an epoxy resin glue.

Now, to make a spring, take about 3" (75mm) of very fine wire like the wire in Chinese spherical lampshades. Double back $\frac{1}{4}$" (6mm) of one end into a flat loop; this goes inside the bird. At a distance of about $\frac{3}{4}$" (18mm) to 1" (25mm) from the loop, begin to bend the rest of the wire closely around the steel post about five or six times, checking to see that the coiled wire will flutter gently down, and is neither too tight nor too loose. The wire should also flutter down in the opposite direction if the stand is inverted. Practice will soon give you the required knack.

When you are satisfied that the spring is working satisfactorily, glue the wire loop into the bird with epoxy resin. Test again that the spring moves well, and cut off any surplus wire at the other end. A bead stuck on the top of the post will prevent the bird from slipping off.

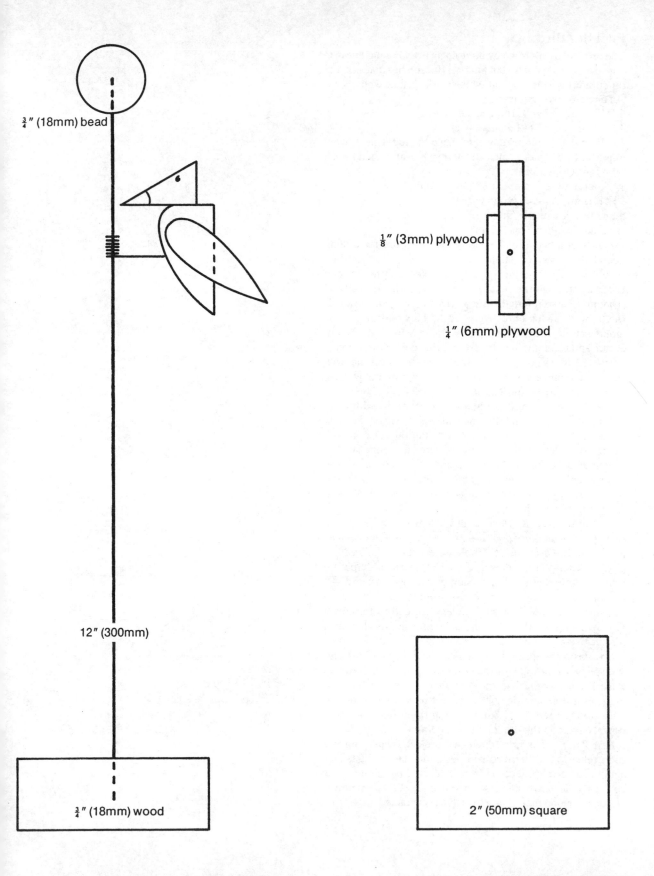

¾″ (18mm) bead

⅛″ (3mm) plywood

¼″ (6mm) plywood

12″ (300mm)

¾″ (18mm) wood

2″ (50mm) square

## Pecking Bird

The original of this toy may have come from Poland because it is so brightly painted, but Michael Hanson has made one of much simpler construction which works just as well.

The materials required are

5" (125mm) of $1\frac{1}{4}$" (31mm) square wood

4" (100mm) of $\frac{1}{2}$" (12.5mm) dowel

1" (25mm) of $\frac{1}{4}$" (6mm) dowel for the bird's leg. This is an all-important little piece; measure it, mark it and round it off with the utmost care!

1" (25mm) of spring about $\frac{3}{8}$" (9mm) wide

$1\frac{1}{4}$" (31mm) of $\frac{1}{16}$" (1.5mm) wire (stiff)

a small piece of $\frac{3}{8}$" (9mm) plywood measuring 4" by 2" (100mm by 50mm) for the bird.

Before you begin, please study the directions for drilling deep holes given for Skippy.

Drill a $\frac{1}{2}$" (12.5mm) diameter hole lengthwise and centrally through the square wood to a depth of exactly 4" (100mm). Make a lengthwise $\frac{3}{4}$" (18mm) long slot towards the front of the top of the wood by marking off three points along a central line at distances of 2", $2\frac{1}{4}$" and $2\frac{1}{2}$" (50mm, 56mm and 62.5mm) from the front. Drill holes at these points with a $\frac{1}{4}$" (6mm) bit and link them together with the drill, knife or file into a slot $\frac{3}{4}$" (18mm) long by $\frac{1}{4}$" (6mm) wide.

Take the 4" (100mm) length of $\frac{1}{2}$" dowel. Drill a hole in the dowel $\frac{1}{4}$" deep (6mm) i.e. half-way through it, with a $\frac{1}{4}$" (6mm) bit $1\frac{1}{4}$" (31mm) from one end, which will be the back — mark it 'B' on the end as a guide during construction. Enlarge the hole so that it slopes towards the front (see the drawing), keeping the tip of the drill at the bottom of the original hole and gradually enlarging the slope towards the front as shown. This should be done carefully with either a hand-drill or a penknife.

Cut out the bird as drawn. Drill a hole with a $\frac{1}{4}$" bit (6mm) *exactly* $\frac{1}{4}$" (6mm) deep into the center of the semi-circular piece (see the drawing); the hole is vertical as the bird sits upright. Glue the leg dowel (the all-important little piece!) into the hole in the bird, having previously drilled a $\frac{1}{16}$" (1.5mm) hole in the foot $\frac{3}{8}$" (9mm) from the bottom, cross-wise through it. (Drill this small hole before cutting the dowel into inch lengths.) Paint the bird in bright colors and varnish him before attaching him in his frame.

Now drop the spring into the deep hole in the frame and then put in the dowel with the hole sloping towards the front. Push it back slightly so that the short dowel on the bird engages in this sloping hole. Secure it there by passing the wire through the $\frac{1}{16}$" (1.5mm) hole in the frame, the short dowel (leg), and the other side of the frame.

Part of the $\frac{1}{2}$" (12.5mm) dowel will project. By pushing and then releasing it, the bird will peck and thump his tail. A small 'dish' can be placed in front of him to hold his food — a counter-sink bit worked a short way into $\frac{3}{4}$" (18mm) dowel or square wood makes an attractive receptacle.

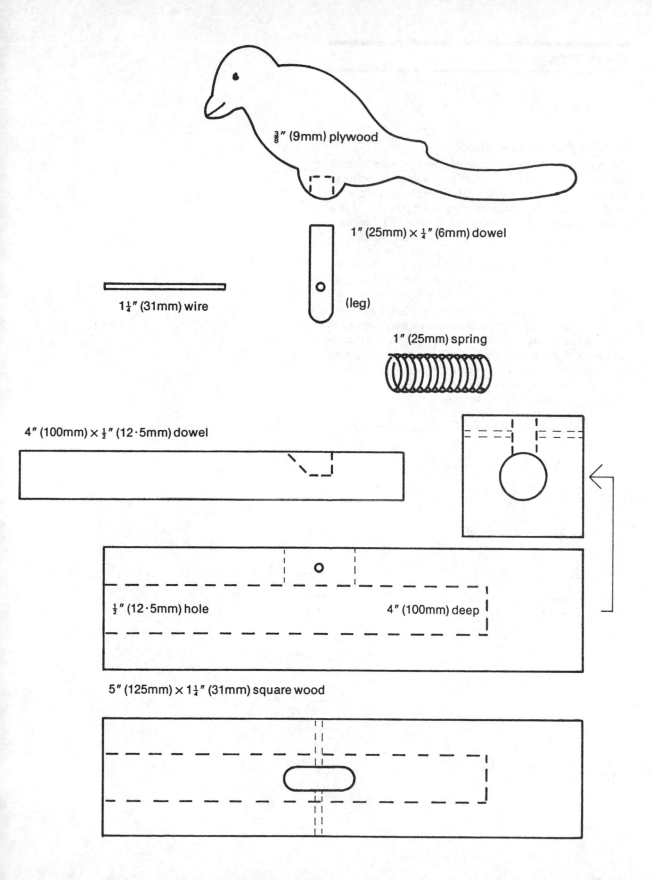

$\frac{3}{8}''$ (9mm) plywood

1" (25mm) × $\frac{1}{4}''$ (6mm) dowel

$1\frac{1}{4}''$ (31mm) wire

(leg)

1" (25mm) spring

4" (100mm) × $\frac{1}{2}''$ (12·5mm) dowel

$\frac{1}{2}''$ (12·5mm) hole

4" (100mm) deep

5" (125mm) × $1\frac{1}{4}''$ (31mm) square wood

# TWISTING

## Twisting-and-Untwisting

This is a simple little toy that people used to make for their children, but which seems to have gone out of fashion. It can be made with a large button and a piece of string — no making in fact — but it is more exciting if it is made of a disc of wood and painted, or, better still, is made in a star-shape because the space between the star's points engenders a pleasant zooming sound which greatly adds to its attraction.

The disc should be between 2″ (50mm) and 3″ (75mm) diameter and cut from about $\frac{1}{4}$″ (6mm) plywood, with two holes drilled one on each side of the center not more than $\frac{1}{2}$″ (12.5mm) apart. The holes should be big enough to let the string through easily. Thread about two yards (1,800mm) of softish string through the holes into a loop, and, with hands held apart, twist the string with the disc in the center, round and round till the string is thoroughly twisted. Then, before it has time to unwind, move your hands towards each other and then out again, and keep on doing this. There is a certain knack in getting the toy working and several attempts may have to be made before it responds, but once it gets going, it could go on for ever!

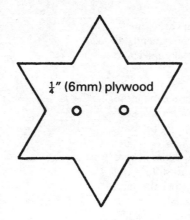

¼″ (6mm) plywood

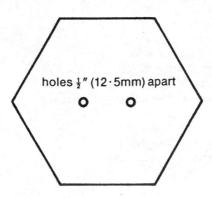

holes ½″ (12·5mm) apart

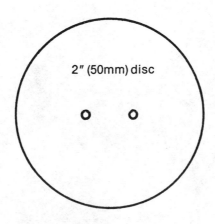

2″ (50mm) disc

## The Acrobat

This is another toy — and it is almost my favorite one — which is motivated by this twisting or torque movement. It is a universal toy, and all countries and all toymakers seem to have their own versions.

The acrobat should be light, made from $\frac{1}{8}''$ (3mm) plywood. His head should not have too high a forehead for the length of his arms or he will not be able to perform properly. His arms and legs should be attached by string, not rivets, to ensure easy movements.

Draw the pattern on thin plywood, drill holes where marked and cut out the pieces. Paint and varnish him and join him together. Make his frame of two pieces of half-round dowel each about 9″ (225mm) long, drilled exactly to match as shown in the drawings. The holes for the screws should be countersunk on the outside. The cross bar can be round dowel or square wood. Use thin screws at least $\frac{1}{2}''$ (12.5mm) long and glue to secure the sides to the bar.

To attach the acrobat to his frame, lay him *away* from it with his head pointing inwards. Put the thread through a lower hole in the frame and an upper hole in his hand, then string on a small bead to keep his hands apart. Then pass the thread through the upper hole in his other hand followed by the lower hole in the opposite side of the frame, and back through the remaining holes. Do not knot the string till you have established the correct length by testing how tight the string should be by applying light pressure on the bottom end of the frame and then releasing it.

The unpredictable aspect of this toy makes it very fascinating. He can perform a great variety of acrobatics, and it is impossible to foretell what he will do next!

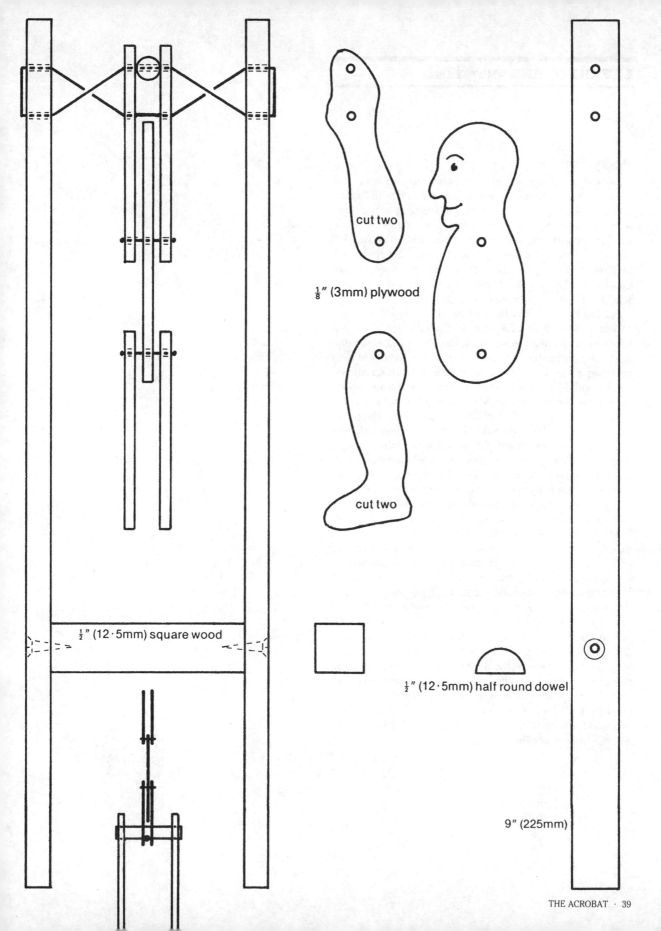

⅛″ (3mm) plywood

cut two

cut two

½″ (12·5mm) square wood

½″ (12·5mm) half round dowel

9″ (225mm)

### Pussy Cat

Pussy Cat developed out of a toy I once saw, where a man popped up out of an apple tree. It is a bit of a *fyke* to explain and to make. If you do not know the meaning of this Scots word, you soon will when you start to make the toy! However, it is a very pleasant toy when it is finished and a good exercise for a toy-maker in exactitude. It intrigues small children as they press the cat's tail down, to see its face appear over the top of the frame, and to discover the mice which had been concealed behind the cat.

Cut out the back and front of the frame together, in $\frac{3}{16}''$ (4.5mm) plywood, and the cat in $\frac{1}{8}''$ (3mm) plywood. Cut out the round and oblong windows in the front by drilling holes inside the perimeter of the wood to be removed and then inserting a saw blade from the inside and cutting around where marked. Lay the front over the back and draw the outlines of the round windows on to the back so that you know where to paint in the mice, which you should do at this point.

Cut two $3\frac{1}{2}''$ (87.5mm) lengths and one $2\frac{1}{4}''$ (56mm) length of $\frac{3}{8}''$ (9mm) square wood. Cut a gap in one of the longer lengths, as shown in the drawings, and glue it along the right-hand side of the back, as the back (with mice) faces you. Glue on the other side length and the shorter bottom length.

Lay the front of the frame over all this, and keep it firm with adhesive or masking tape. Drill a $\frac{1}{4}''$ (6mm) diameter hole from front to back of the right-hand edge of the frame, exactly as marked i.e. with the centre $1\frac{3}{4}''$ (43mm) from top and $\frac{1}{4}''$ (6mm) from edge, slipping a piece of wood into the gap as support while doing so.

At or before this stage, cut out and drill the cat's tail. Drill a $\frac{1}{4}''$ (6mm) hole in the center of the cat's body as shown in the drawings, $\frac{1}{2}''$ (12.5mm) from the bottom. Now, paint the cat and its tail. When the paint has dried, glue a tiny piece of dowel into the hole drilled in the cat's body about $\frac{3}{8}''$ (9mm) long and let it project at the back of the cat. Now slip the tail through the slot in the side of the frame and engage the cat on it. Ensure that you can move the cat up and down satisfactorily, and, if so, glue on the front and glue in a short piece of dowel from the back or front, catching the tail in position, and the toy is complete.

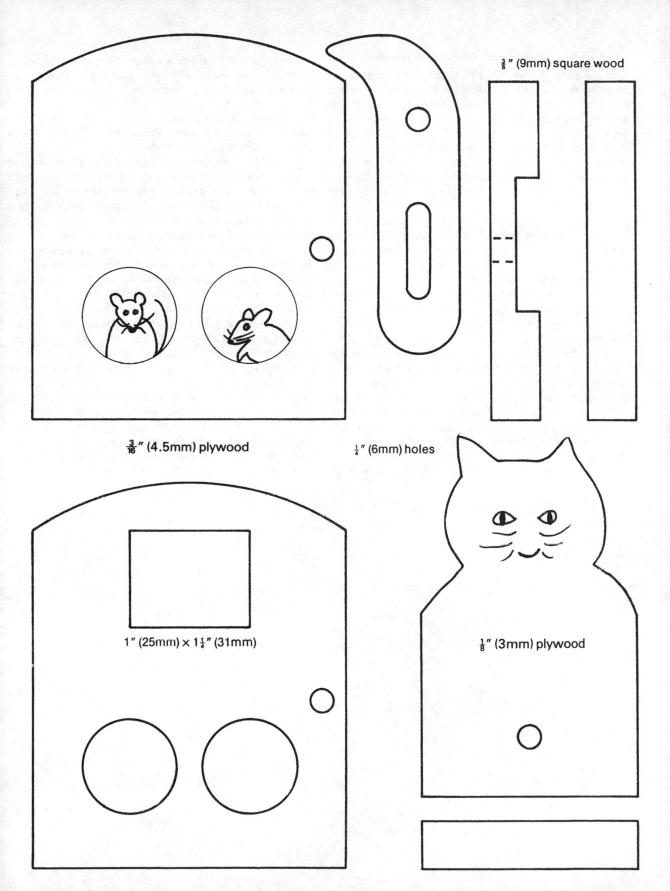

$\frac{3}{8}''$ (9mm) square wood

$\frac{3}{16}''$ (4.5mm) plywood

$\frac{1}{4}''$ (6mm) holes

1" (25mm) × 1$\frac{1}{4}$" (31mm)

$\frac{1}{8}''$ (3mm) plywood

## Men at Work or Tom, Dick and Harry

This toy I also discovered in Majorca and I think it is of Spanish origin. It bears out my theory that if the movement of a toy is understood, new versions can be evolved. This toy, although so different in appearance to the familiar pecking hens, is made exactly on the same principle, and is most diverting. The original is rather cynical, black and slightly sinister, though it is brilliantly executed, so I have made a new version with much more cheerful smiling chaps, and have also made other alterations to give a pleasanter effect for children.

In making this toy, great attention must be paid to detail. If, for instance, the arms are too short or the drill hole for the hammer placed too far back, then the handle cannot swing properly. With care, it is not at all difficult to make successfully, and it is a very clever, enjoyable toy.

Cut out the platform in thin $\frac{1}{8}''$ (3mm) plywood and drill the holes exactly as shown in the drawings. Cut out the table and its base and glue them together, and then glue the table into position.

Cut out the little men — do not make them any fatter in front or the handles of the hammers will catch on their 'tummies'! Drill the tiny holes in the arms before cutting them out, then, having cut them out, glue them carefully into position as marked, making sure the holes are in line. Paint and varnish them. Draw the handles of the hammers on to $\frac{1}{8}''$ (3mm) plywood, drilling the two holes required in each before cutting, so as to avoid the risk of splitting.

Similarly, mark off $\frac{1}{2}''$ (12.5mm) spaces along a $\frac{1}{2}''$ (12.5mm) dowel for the heads of the hammers, and, before cutting out the heads, drill a $\frac{3}{16}''$ (4.5mm) hole through the center of each about $\frac{1}{4}''$ (6mm) deep, supporting the dowel on each side with a clamp to prevent it splitting. Glue the handles into the heads, taking care that the holes for wire and thread are sideways up. Thread about 20" (500mm) of strong thread into the end holes.

Cut $1\frac{1}{2}''$ (37.5mm) lengths of thin but firm and easily-bent wire. Bend it over at one end to make a small loop to prevent the wire from slipping out. Put it through one hand, through the handle of the hammer and then through the other hand of each little man in turn; at the same time, pass the ends of the threads on the hammers into their respective holes.

Now, test the position of each little man to ensure that his hammer rests on the table — the threads are in a direct line through the holes in the platform — and that no hammer interferes with any other. When this is established, put a pencil mark around each man and glue him into position. A piece of plywood with a heavy weight on top of it is a good way to press them when glued. Close up the other ends of the wires which carry the hammers.

When they are firmly set, test by pulling the threads that all is in working order. Then turn the toy upside down, and, getting all threads evenly positioned, join them loosely together (while you are experimenting) about 2" (50mm) below the platform. Attach the remainder of the thread to a largish bead or cube about 4" (100mm) away, and make your own adjustments, and this delightful toy should be complete and in good working order.

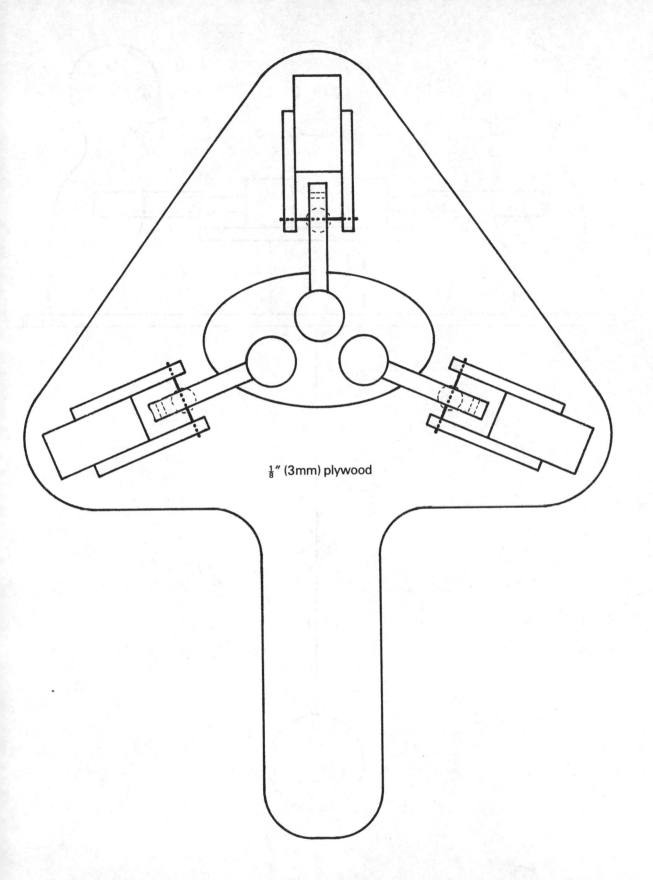

$\frac{1}{8}''$ (3mm) plywood

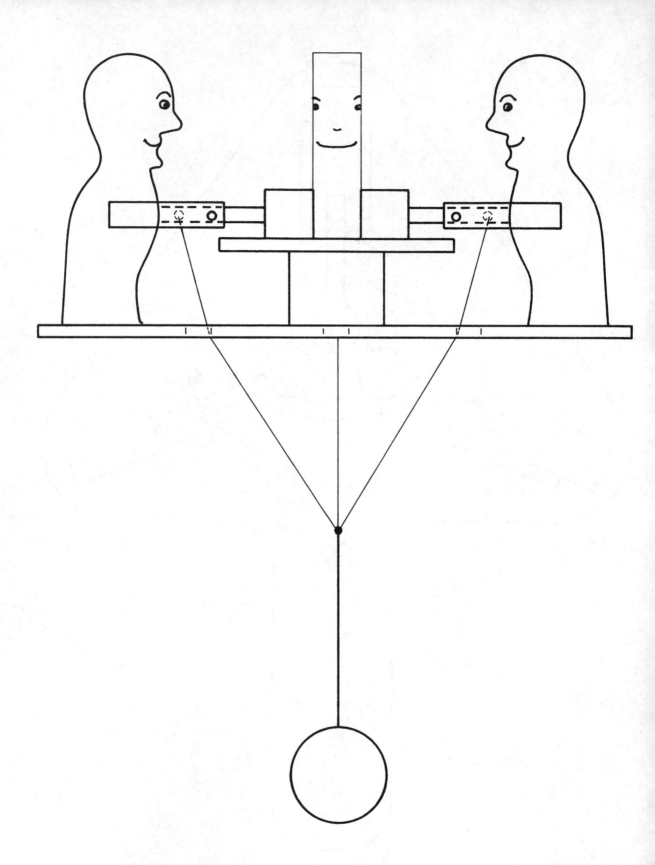

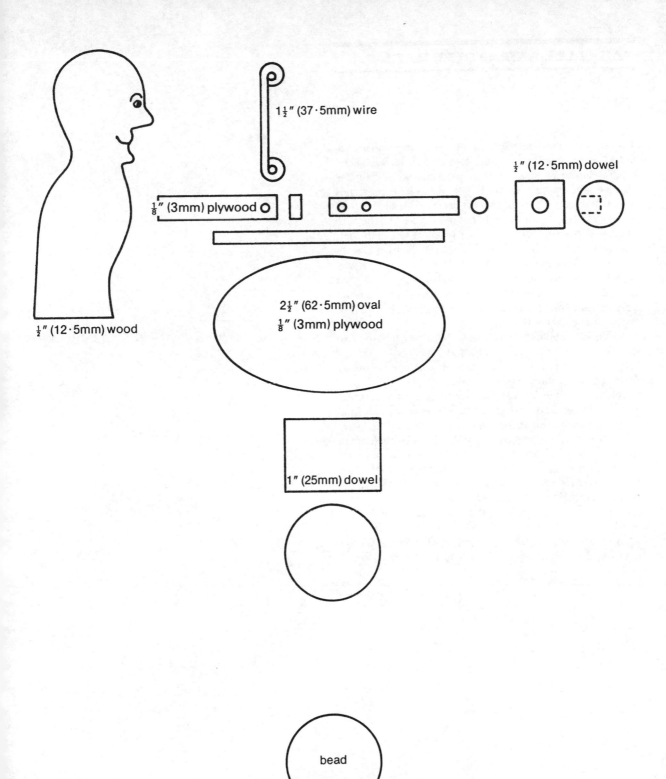

1½″ (37·5mm) wire

½″ (12·5mm) dowel

⅛″ (3mm) plywood

2½″ (62·5mm) oval
⅛″ (3mm) plywood

½″ (12·5mm) wood

1″ (25mm) dowel

bead

# PARALLEL AND ANGLED BARS

The use of parallel bars to produce movement in toys is well-known and many fine examples come to us from Russia and Central Europe. In many of these toys a man with a hammer stands at one end of a bar, and a bear with a hammer stands at the other end. These figures are attached by a loose rivet either to the same side of the bar in some cases or if they are made with two legs each, with a leg on either side of the bar.

Above this bar, a second bar, drilled with holes in exactly the same places as the first one, is placed the opposite way round, so that the ends of the bars overlap at each end when the holes are in a perpendicular line. A block of wood or an anvil is glued on the upper bar in a position calculated to receive the blows of the hammers.

An equally popular variant is to have two men or two dwarfs sawing through a log of wood.

In many cases the figures are placed an inch or two away from the end of the bar (see drawing).

This toy is not difficult to make but requires great exactitude. The holes in the bars must be in line horizontally and perpendicularly, and at the same distance from the center.

The bars must be set exactly parallel to each other, about $\frac{1}{8}''$ (3mm) or $\frac{1}{4}''$ (6mm) apart when the figures are in their upright position. Both figures are loosely riveted to the bars to allow them the maximum amount of movement when the bars are pushed to and fro. It is important to remember that the toy works best when the figures are small and not far apart.

Three examples of this movement used in different ways are given here, Ding Dong, The Goats, and the Brothers.

## Ding Dong

Ding Dong emerged one day when I was making a sawing men toy. It all happened when I took away their saw and discovered a wonderful arm movement in consequence. As the resulting effect could easily look like fighting, which would be undesirable, I gave my little men something else to do. I tied a bead loosely on to each hand, fixed a metal lid or disc on to a post on the upper bar, mid-way between them, thus enabling them to bang away to the heart's content of anyone who set them in motion.

In another version of this toy which I call Whirligig, the men succeed in turning a wheel around. Another pair can raise and low a scissor frame-work with a star at the end. Directions for these toys are not given here, they are only mentioned to show that there is considerable scope for improvisation on this movement.

To make Ding Dong proceed as follows:—

Draw the little men with the strip under their front feet and their two arms on to a piece of $\frac{3}{16}$" (4.5mm) plywood, and mark in the holes for rivets. Lay this plywood over a similar piece and strap them together. Drill the holes and cut out the shapes, paint and varnish them, rivet the arms loosely to the bodies and tie a bead on to each of their hands.

Prepare their frame by taking two bars of any type of hardwood $\frac{3}{16}$" (4.5mm) thick, $\frac{3}{4}$" (18mm) wide and 12" (300m) long. Drill them as shown in the drawing so that the space between the figures will be 7" (175mm). On one bar, mark the mid-point between the drill holes i.e. $3\frac{1}{2}$" (87.5mm) and glue a $1\frac{1}{2}$" (37.5mm) strip of the same wood over each side. This is to enable you to drill in centrally a post of $\frac{3}{8}$" (9mm) dowel, $1\frac{1}{4}$" (31mm) long, previously drilled with a $\frac{1}{8}$" (3mm) hole to take a $\frac{1}{2}$" (12.5mm) rivet.

With an $\frac{1}{8}$" (3mm) bit drill through the center of a small tin lid of about $2\frac{3}{4}$" (68mm) diameter and fix it loosely on to the post with an $\frac{1}{8}$" (3mm) rivet glued into the hole.

Now rivet the men loosely on to their bars, both on the same side, and set them to work, ding dong!

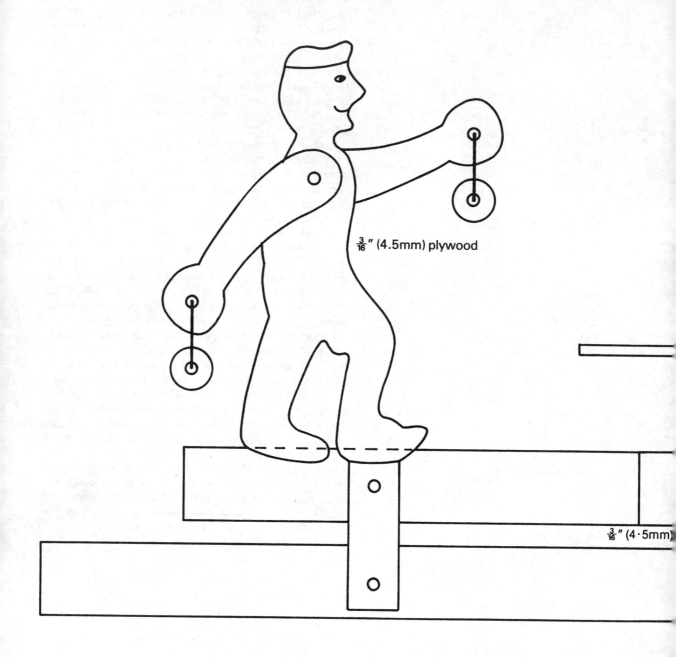

$\frac{3}{16}''$ (4.5mm) plywood

$\frac{3}{16}''$ (4·5mm)

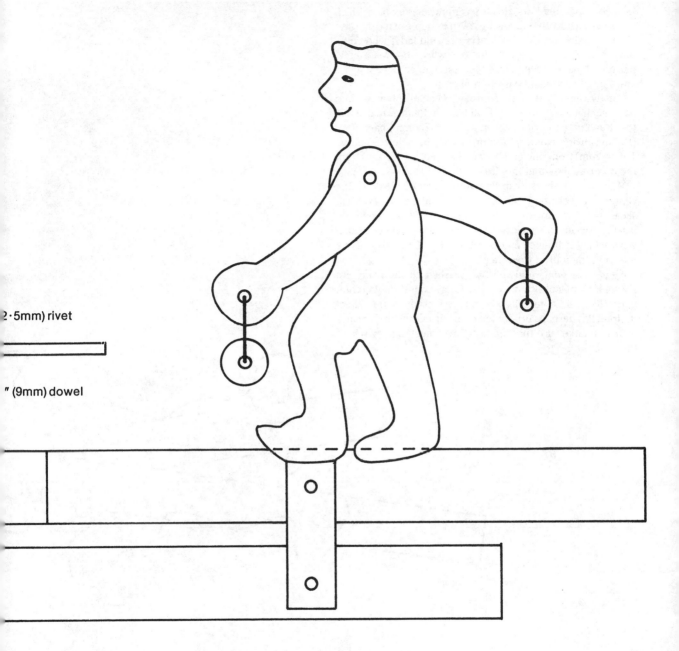

2·5mm) rivet

″ (9mm) dowel

## The Goats

Instead of parallel bars, this toy is motivated by bars which cross over each other at an angle. An example of it came into my possession on the death of a very old lady, who could have had it made specially for her when she was a child because I have never come across another one. It is an amusing little toy and easy to make.

Cut two identical goats from $\frac{3}{16}$" (4.5mm) plywood and paint each a different color. Drill holes in them as marked in the drawing, and drill holes in two 10" (250mm) bars of $\frac{1}{2}$" (15.5mm) wide wood $\frac{1}{8}$" (3mm) thick. The holes should be $1\frac{3}{4}$" (43mm) from one end of each bar and $2\frac{1}{4}$" (56mm) from the other as shown in the drawing.

Make two washers by drilling an $\frac{1}{8}$" (3mm) hole down the center of a piece of $\frac{1}{2}$" (12.5mm) dowel and cutting off two slices $\frac{3}{16}$" (4.5mm) thick. Both washers will be needed to insert between the back bar and that part of the goats' anatomy which is affected by the cross-over, i.e. the back of one goat and the foot of the other.

Attach the goats and the two washers to the bars with rivets, making sure that they clash head on. If they do not, alter the drill holes slightly till you produce the effect desired. It is perhaps prudent to make up this toy first in cardboard to make sure that the heads will meet exactly where they should.

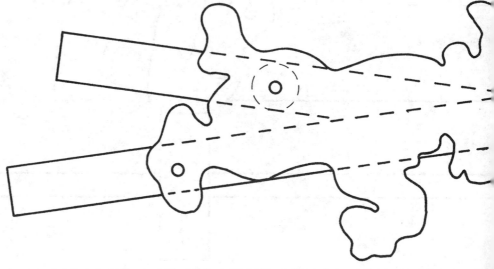

$\frac{1}{8}$" (3mm)

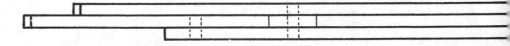

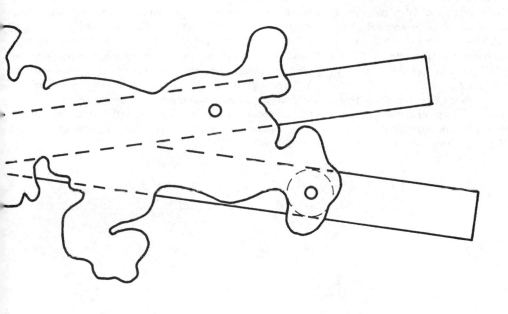

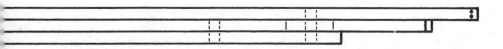

## Brothers

The third toy in this section is motivated by parallel bars inserted between thick discs. The idea came from a drawing of a folk toy in which a peasant woman and a goose apparently take it in turn to chase each other. I have changed them into two seated figures with movable arms and legs and call them Brothers: like most brothers — and sisters — they sometimes want to confide in each other and sometimes prefer to go their own way. The mechanism is not too easy to explain, but it is very satisfactory when it is working and the drawings should make it quite clear.

The following items are required to make this toy:

Four 2″ (50mm) disc $\frac{1}{2}$″ (12.5mm) thick

Two pieces of $\frac{3}{4}$″ (18mm) wide ramin (hard wood) $\frac{3}{16}$″ (4.5mm) thick, 9″ (225mm) long. These bars are to be rounded at each end, drilled with $\frac{3}{16}$″ (4.5mm) holes 4″ (100mm) apart, $3\frac{1}{2}$ (87.5mm) from one end and $1\frac{1}{2}$″ (37.5mm) from the other end.

Six pegs 1″ (25mm) long of $\frac{3}{16}$″ (4.5mm) dowel.

Two small pieces of $\frac{3}{8}$″ (9mm) plywood for the brothers

Eight small pieces of $\frac{1}{8}$″ (3mm) plywood for their arms and legs.

Draw a diametrical line across one side of each disc, and then with a radius of $\frac{3}{4}$″ (18mm) draw an inner circle on all four of them. At the two points on each disc where the inner circle cuts the diameters, drill holes with a $\frac{3}{16}$″ (4.5mm) drill $\frac{3}{8}$″ (9mm) deep, so as not to pierce right through the disc, for the sake of appearance only. Insert one end of four of the 1″ (25mm) pegs into two of the discs.

Fit the bars over the four pegs in the two discs so that a long end overlaps right and left. Fit the other discs on top of the other ends of the pegs but for the moment do not glue them in place. This will already give you a toy with a pleasant movement, with the bars controlled by the discs alternately closing together and then pushing apart to become close together again in the opposite direction.

Cut two little men out of $\frac{3}{8}$″ (9mm) plywood, plus two arms and two legs for each, out of $\frac{1}{8}$″ (3mm) plywood, drilling holes as marked before cutting. Then make a hole $\frac{1}{2}$″ (12.5mm) deep with a $\frac{3}{16}$″ (4.5mm) drill in the bottom of each body about $\frac{1}{4}$″ (6mm) from the front.

Paint and varnish these loose parts. When dry, rivet the arms and legs loosely on to the bodies. Now, with the bars in a closed position, set the little men opposite to each other on their discs. Calculate the spots for fixing them there with the pegs from their bodies, which will be at a point along a line immediately above where the bars touch. Drill holes $\frac{1}{2}$″ (12.5mm) deep in the tops of the discs at these points and insert the two remaining 1″ (25mm) pegs into the holes to connect with the holes in the bodies.

Test that everything is now in working order. If it is, glue the pegs on the discs into position with the bars between them. Glue the little men on to their pegs and, after applying glue over their bottoms and their pegs, fix them on to their seats to complete the toy.

This is an original toy which I devised and I think you will find it easy to make and fascinating to play with, and it may inspire you to develop a version of your own!

The fact that the arms and legs can be moved independently gives additional interest to the toy. The limbs can be used to express a variety of moods, so the riveting must be loose enough to allow movement, but firm enough for the limbs to stay in place when moved. Care must be taken to see that hands and feet cannot overlap and that the feet cannot drop below the platform, or the movement will be hampered.

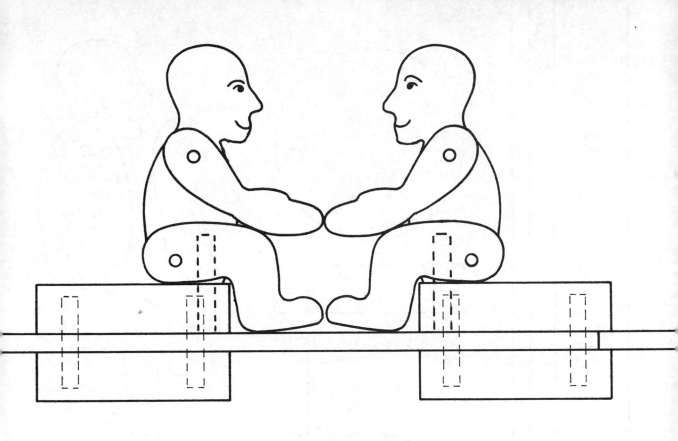

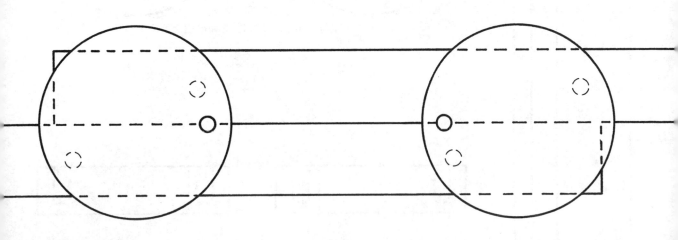

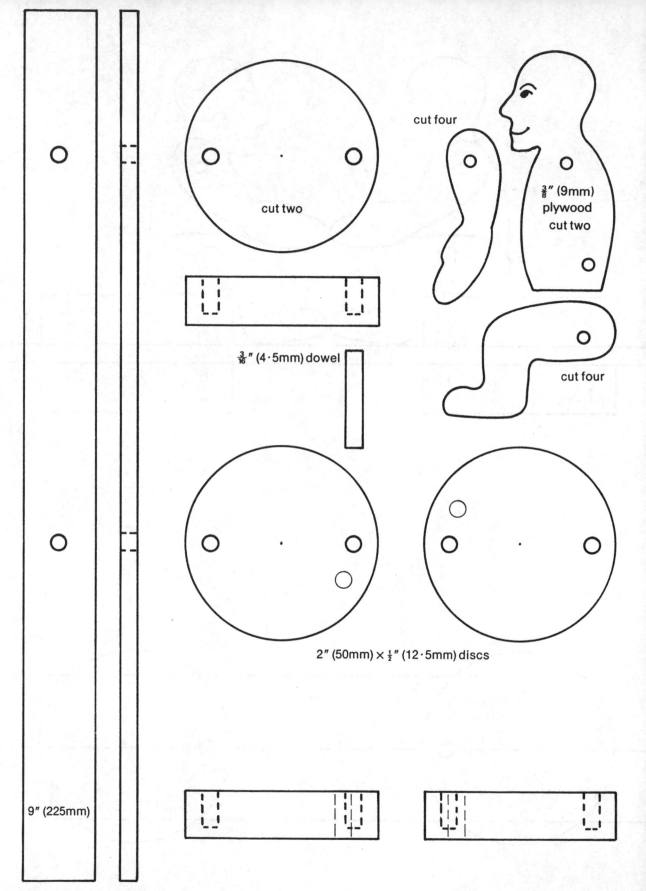

cut four

$\frac{3}{8}$" (9mm) plywood cut two

cut two

cut four

$\frac{3}{16}$" (4·5mm) dowel

2" (50mm) × $\frac{1}{2}$" (12·5mm) discs

9" (225mm)

# BENT-AXLE TOYS

A bent axle is a device used by toymakers to produce movements in a toy as it is wheeled along. The axle, made of fairly stiff wire, has a square loop made in it, generally in the center. To this loop is attached a wire which is connected at the other end with a moving limb, say a leg, an arm or the head of a figure. Alternatively, this device can be used to produce movement in an animal placed on a cart on wheels. A hole is cut in the bottom of the card to allow the bent axle free movement. The ends of the axle pass through the undercarriage and are pressed into thick, usually rather large wheels, and firmly fixed. As the wheels revolve, so the bent axle revolves, pulling with it the wire to which the movable limb has been attached. In the example given here, a duck moves its head up and down making a clacking noise at the same time. Very many variations on this theme have been made and there are surely many more which can easily be devised.

It is a good idea to start by learning how to make bent axles if you do not already know the technique. No doubt there are several methods, but the following suggestions may help. Suppose the bent axle is to be this size when finished, i.e. its total length is $1\frac{1}{2}''$ (37.5mm) plus $1\frac{1}{2}''$ plus $1\frac{1}{2}''$.

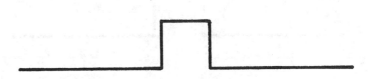

Take 5″ (125mm) length of wire and mark the center point A, and points B and C $\frac{1}{4}''$ (6mm) each side of it.

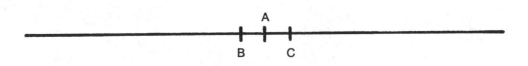

Bend the wire at right angles at B and C. Draw the ends through a piece of $\frac{1}{2}''$ (12.5mm) wood, in which you have drilled two holes $\frac{1}{2}''$ (12.5mm) apart.

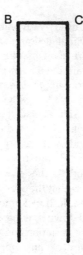

Hammer BAC flat to the wood, and then bend the ends of the wire at right angles back along the wood at X and Y and press the wood in a vice.

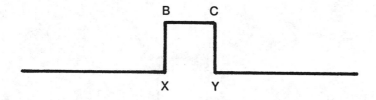

With a saw and pliers, cut away the wood and there should remain a perfect bent axle! Cut away any surplus wire at each end.

## Quacking Duck

The Duck is a push-along toy whose neck and head are connected by a wire to a loop in the wire of the axle, i.e. a bent axle, so that the wire moves his neck forward and back as the wheels revolve. In the design given, the nape of the neck hits against the duck's back making a most satisfactory knocking sound, rather like the quack of a duck.

Cut two wings as shown from $\frac{1}{4}''$ (6mm) plywood and drill holes where marked, a $\frac{1}{4}''$ (6mm) hole for the short dowel which holds the neck in place, and a $\frac{1}{8}''$ (3mm) hole for the wire axle to go through. Cut the neck and head as shown and the small piece for the back from $\frac{3}{4}''$ (18mm) wood. Drill a $\frac{1}{4}''$ (6mm) hole through the neck where shown, and two very small holes in the back of the neck where marked to take a small staple. The staple must be knocked in firmly, but ensure that enough of the loop is left for the wire to be hooked on to it.

Make a bent axle from $\frac{1}{8}''$ (3mm) wire as shown, and a connecting rod with a hook at each end from $\frac{1}{16}''$ (1.5mm) wire. Cut two wheels of 2'' (50mm) diameter from $\frac{1}{2}''$ (12.5mm) thick wood. Drill a hole in the center $\frac{1}{4}''$ (6mm) deep with a $\frac{1}{8}''$ (3mm) drill to take the axle; do not drill them right through.

Hold the back in a vice or clamp to prevent it from splitting and drill a $\frac{3}{8}''$ (9mm) hole through it to a depth of $\frac{1}{2}''$ (12.5mm) at an angle of about 40 degrees, as marked. Glue the back on to one wing.

Paint and varnish the toy at this stage. When dry, assemble as follows but do not glue anything until you are certain everything is going to work. Hook the wire to the staple on the neck and close the hook with pliers. Put a $1\frac{1}{4}''$ (31mm) length of $\frac{1}{4}''$ (6mm) dowel through the neck and through the wing which has just been glued to the back. Attach the other end of the wire to the bend in the axle and put the end of the axle through the small hole in the wing. Place the other wing in position over the dowel in the neck and the axle wire.

Hold the duck in the back with your finger and thumb, and test, by moving the bent axle with your other hand, that the mechanism is correctly adjusted, that the wire is long enough to allow the axle free play and the head is moving satisfactorily.

If all is in order, glue the second wing to the back and glue the dowel into the holes in the wings to keep the neck in place. Work Rapid Araldite (epoxy resin) into the holes in the wheels and attach them to the ends of the axle, and leave them to set. A touch of Araldite on the top corners of the loop ensures that the hook does not slip off again.

Glue a bead as a hand-hold on to an 18'' (450mm) long dowel of $\frac{3}{8}''$ (9mm) diameter and glue the other end into the back of the duck, and now you should have a delightful, gently quacking, push-along duck!

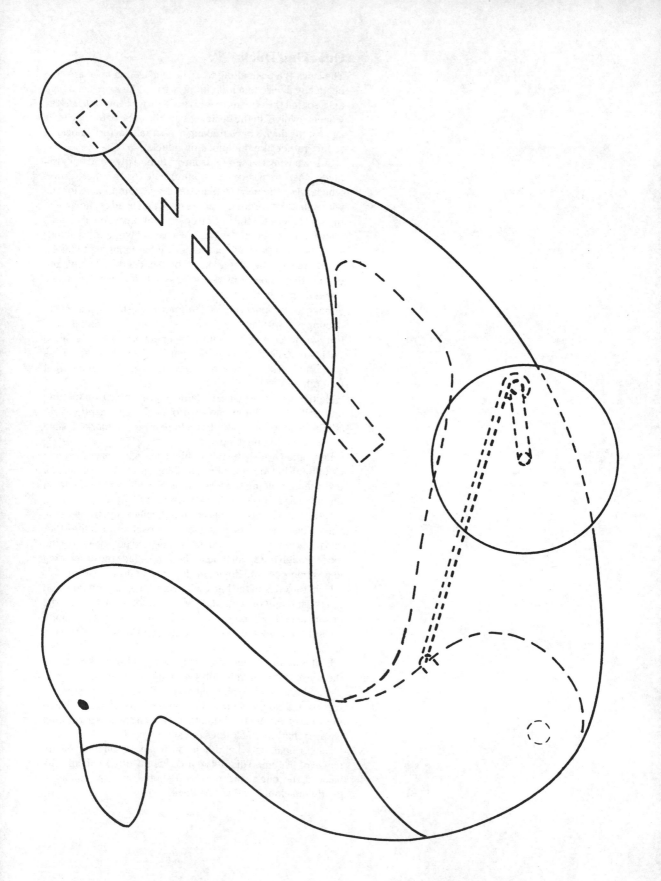

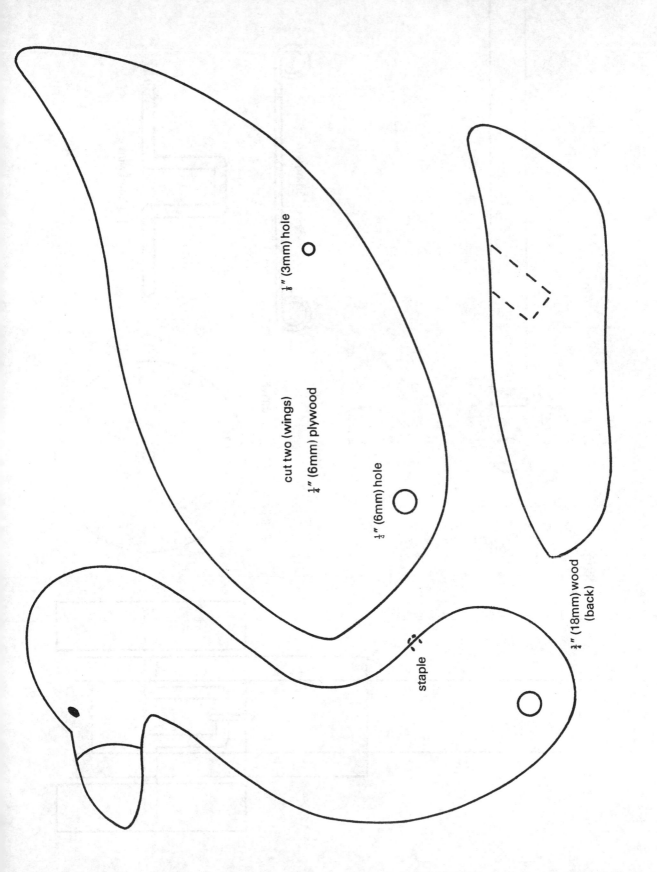

cut two (wings)

$\frac{1}{8}$" (3mm) hole

$\frac{1}{4}$" (6mm) plywood

$\frac{1}{4}$" (6mm) hole

staple

$\frac{3}{4}$" (18mm) wood (back)

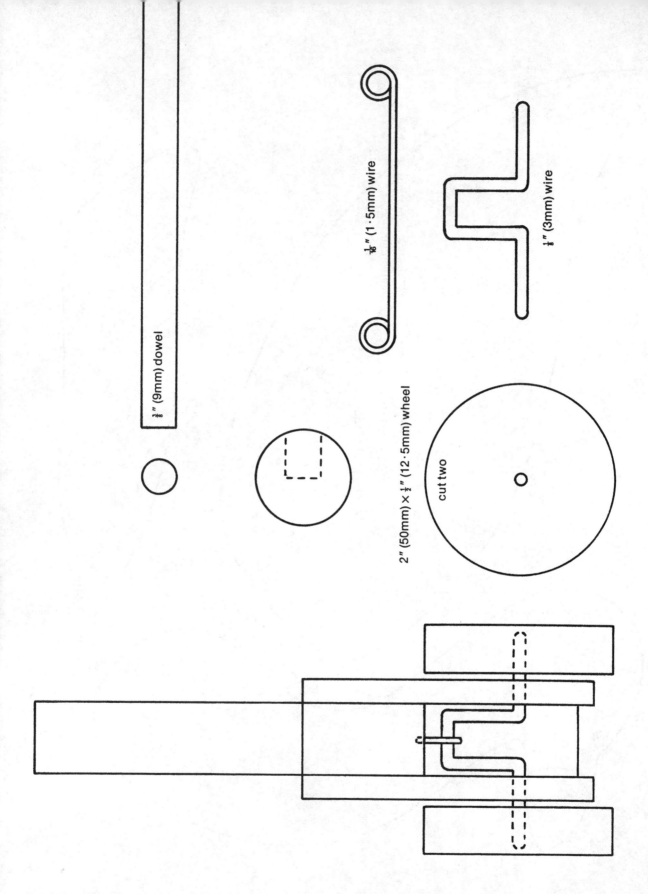

$\frac{3}{8}$" (9mm) dowel

$\frac{1}{16}$" (1·5mm) wire

$\frac{1}{8}$" (3mm) wire

2" (50mm) × $\frac{1}{2}$" (12·5mm) wheel

cut two

# CAM MOVEMENT

## Jemima

A somewhat battered, incomplete toy-crane came my way from a rummage sale. It had a rather fascinating movement, almost like that of a bent-axle but much easier to make. The movement is produced by a device called a cam. The dictionary definition of a cam by the way is 'an eccentric projection on a revolving shaft shaped so as to give some desired linear motion to another part.' I have used the movement to produce a quite different toy, Jemima, a friendly sort of dinosaur, which is interesting and quite simple to make and fun for a small child to play with.

Drill and cut out the two sides as shown. Glue Jemima's neck to her body, matching the pivot holes. Cut out the four 2" (50mm) diameter wheels from $\frac{1}{2}$" (12.5mm) thick wood, or get them turned, and drill a $\frac{3}{8}$" (9mm) hole into, but, for appearance, not right through their centers. The cam is made from a 1" (25mm) length of $\frac{7}{8}$" (22mm) dowel, through which a $\frac{3}{8}$" (9mm) hole is carefully drilled slightly off center.

Test that the toy is working by putting it together in the following way. Position the cam on to the center of the front axle. Make sure that the cam cannot slip, and, if necessary, bind transparent or masking tape on the center of the axle to make it grip. Now put one end of this axle through one of the sides from the inside front, and, at the same time, put one end of the pivot into its hole on the same side, again from the inside. Add a washer to the pivot, then Jemima, and then the other washer. Next, fit the other side, simultaneously fitting it over the pivot and the other end of the front axle. Note that the axles and pivot bar will protrude. Keep the sides in place with a rubber band. Slip in the back axle. Put all four wheels on.

Test the movement. If it is satisfactory, take Jemima to pieces again and paint and varnish all parts, and make any necessary adjustments. When the parts are dry, put the toy together again, gluing the wheels on to their axles, and glue in the small bar at the top to strengthen the frame.

Slip a yard (metre) or slightly more of string through the small holes in front, add a bell, and a bead as hand-hold, and off goes Jemima! If, gentle reader, you like the movement and do not particularly like Jemima, you might be interested to turn the toy back into a crane again, or into something totally different!

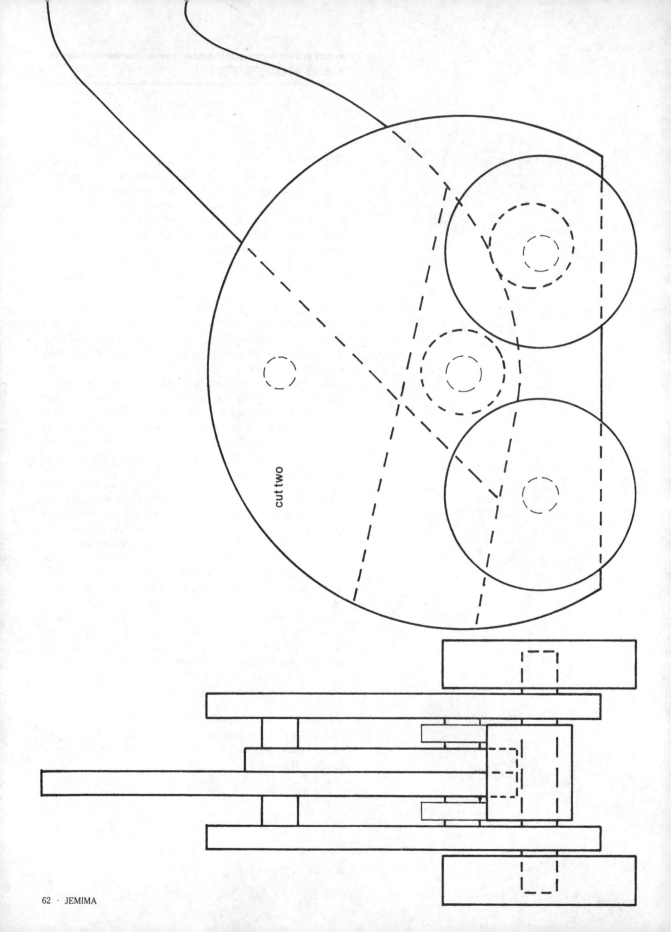

cut two

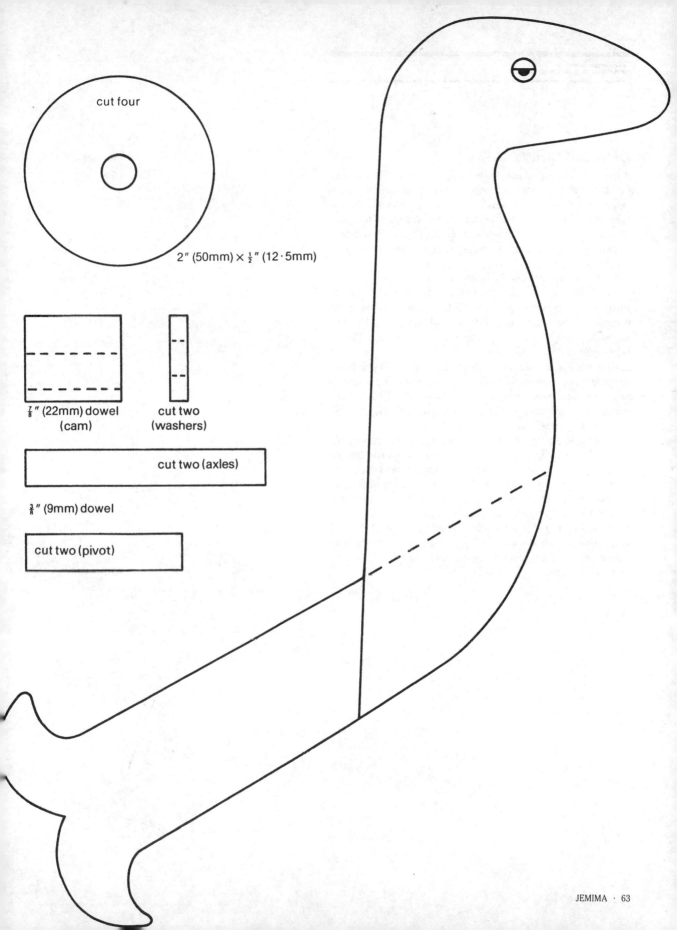

cut four

2" (50mm) × ½" (12·5mm)

⅞" (22mm) dowel
(cam)

cut two
(washers)

cut two (axles)

⅜" (9mm) dowel

cut two (pivot)

# JOINTING

## Dolls and Giraffe

Small children enjoy playing with jointed toys. They like to be able to manipulate them into different attitudes. It seems to give them a sense of power when the toy does what it is told and stays put. This is especially the case, I think, with spastic children, who, unable to control their own limbs, experience satisfaction in controlling the movements of their toy.

From the distant past, I can remember how very funny it seemed when my long-legged Dutch doll was made to wade through a glass bowl containing fish, which scattered in all directions. This was a treat I was very seldom allowed, on the humanitarian grounds that it was cruel to the fish: but I certainly enjoyed the spectacle!

Two examples of jointed toys are given here. The dolls do not need any explanation. They can of course be made in any size. The arms and legs should be attached loosely enough to allow easy manipulation, but tight enough for the doll to stay in position.

The giraffe was made several years ago when very many people in different lands were concerned with the fate of Victor, a giraffe at Marwell Zoo. He collapsed, and could not be got on to his feet again. His long legs and long neck, and somewhat curious anatomy, make him an ideal subject for manipulating. The drawings make it quite clear, I think, how he is put together. The tail is made of string, about 3″ (75mm) long, glued in as shown, with the last inch stranded and painted black. This principle of jointing could be applied in many directions.

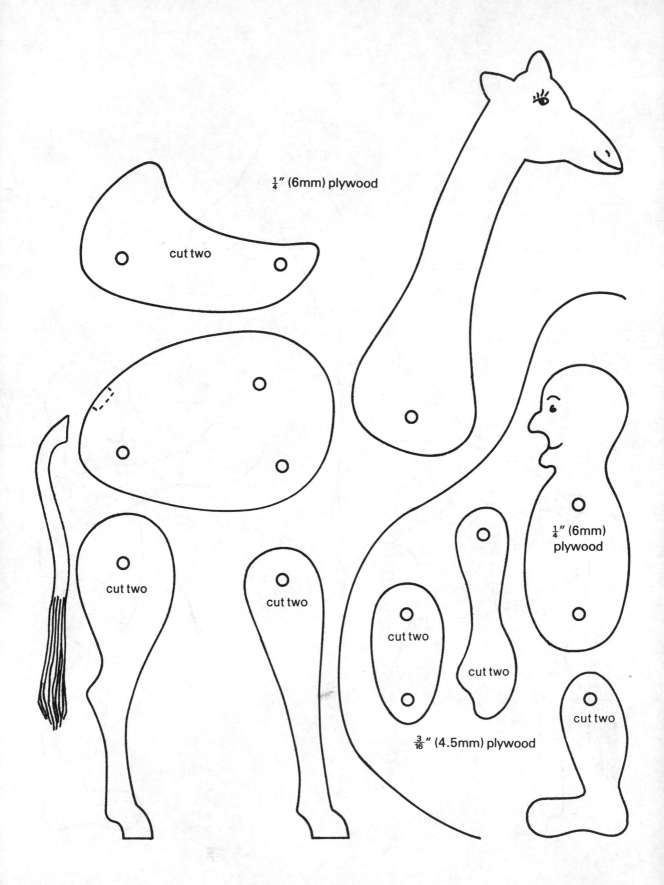

¼" (6mm) plywood

cut two

cut two

cut two

cut two

cut two

¼" (6mm) plywood

cut two

cut two

³⁄₁₆" (4.5mm) plywood

## The Snake

This toy was worked out, and drawn, by Michael Hanson from sections of a realistic bamboo snake found by my son at a rummage sale. Take a length of bamboo with thinnish walls and cut it into pieces 2″ (50mm) and 3″ (75mm) long. About seven pieces is a good number, using the narrower and smaller ones for the head and tail ends, and the larger ones for the body. Draw rounded points at the top and bottom of each piece, opposite to each other as shown, and saw them into shape according to the diagram. Drill small holes in these top and bottom projections, so that the wire which connects each piece to the next will be running at a slight angle, as shown. The wires can be secured either by twisting them into a loop at each end, or by attaching a small bead each end with Araldite (epoxy resin).

The movement of the Snake is very realistic. If you are holding it near the tail, be careful it does not turn round and bite you! The illusion is much increased by suitable painting.

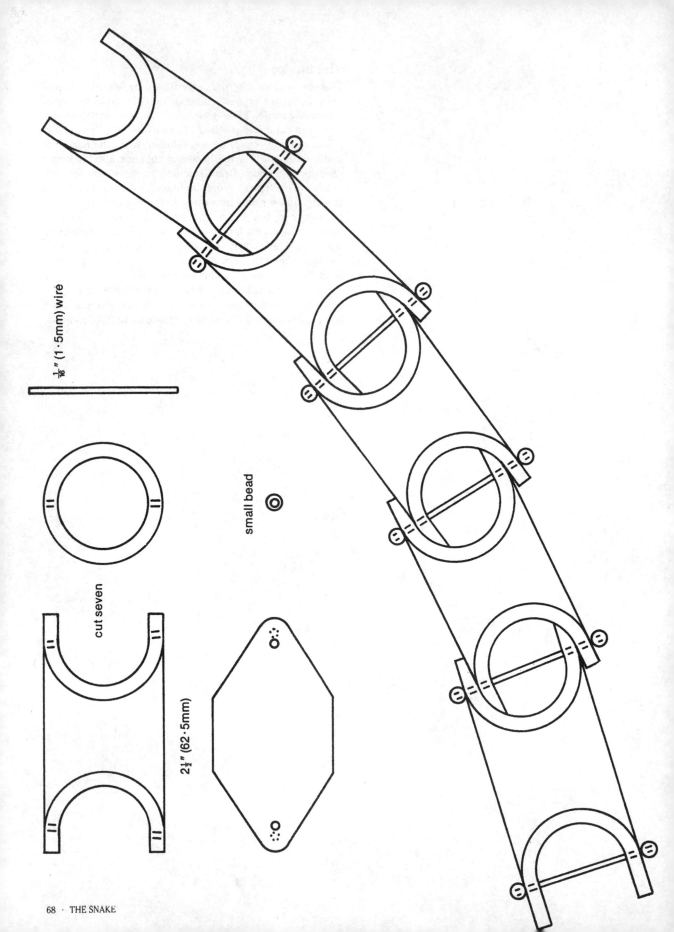

$\frac{1}{16}$" (1·5mm) wire

small bead

cut seven

$2\frac{1}{2}$" (62·5mm)

# BALANCING

## Spinning Jenny

Spinning Jenny is my version of a well-known balance toy. In response to a gentle turn on the rod which goes through Jenny, and which she seems to be holding, she will move backwards or forwards along parallel lines.

In my first book (*Wooden Toys that Work*), she had a short run in a frame which could be converted into a table. This rather cramped her style, and now I recommend making two end-pieces of $\frac{3}{4}''$ (18mm) wood, 6" × 6" (150mm × 150mm); or else of thinner wood with blocks added to support it. In these end-pieces, holes are drilled with centers $2\frac{1}{2}''$ (62.5mm) apart and $1\frac{1}{2}''$ (37.5mm) from the top, to carry two lengths of $\frac{3}{8}''$ (9mm) or $\frac{1}{2}''$ (12.5mm) dowel approximately 3' (900mm) long. She would of course spin right across a room if she had enough length of dowel to support her! It is not necessary to glue the rods into the end pieces, so the toy can be dismantled and put away after use.

As well as spinning straight along, Jenny will climb a gentle slope made by resting one end-piece on a book, and then come back again of her own accord. It has been found that this toy has a socializing effect on children working on it from opposite ends. If Jenny is spun too fast and knocks up against the end, she will stop altogether, but if the end is lifted at the right moment, she will return and can be kept going backwards and forwards indefinitely. This requires skill and judgment on the part of the operators to assess the right moment when to interrupt her progress, and how steep or how shallow should be the angle of the dowels she is spinning along, for, if they are too steep, Jenny can only slither.

In another, very simple, smaller variation of this toy, I use two $3\frac{1}{2}''$ (87.5mm) long bars of $\frac{3}{4}''$ (18mm) wood, with two $\frac{3}{16}''$ (4.5mm) holes drilled in them 2" (50mm) apart. These bars or end-pieces are connected with each other by two lengths of $\frac{3}{16}''$ (4.5mm) dowel about 18" (450mm) long, which can either be glued in or be left loose as you choose. It takes quite a lot of practice and skill to keep the figure turning steadily for say twenty or more times without putting in a helping hand. What about a hundred times?

A smaller Jack or Jenny reigns over this frame, and he or she is the correct size for Tapsalteerie, the next toy. The all important point in a balance toy of this kind is to find the center of gravity. Michael Hanson has worked out simple instructions on how to do this, and you may find it interesting to experiment for yourself in making different figures.

$\frac{3}{16}''$ (4.5mm) plywood

$\frac{3}{16}''$ (4·5mm) dowel

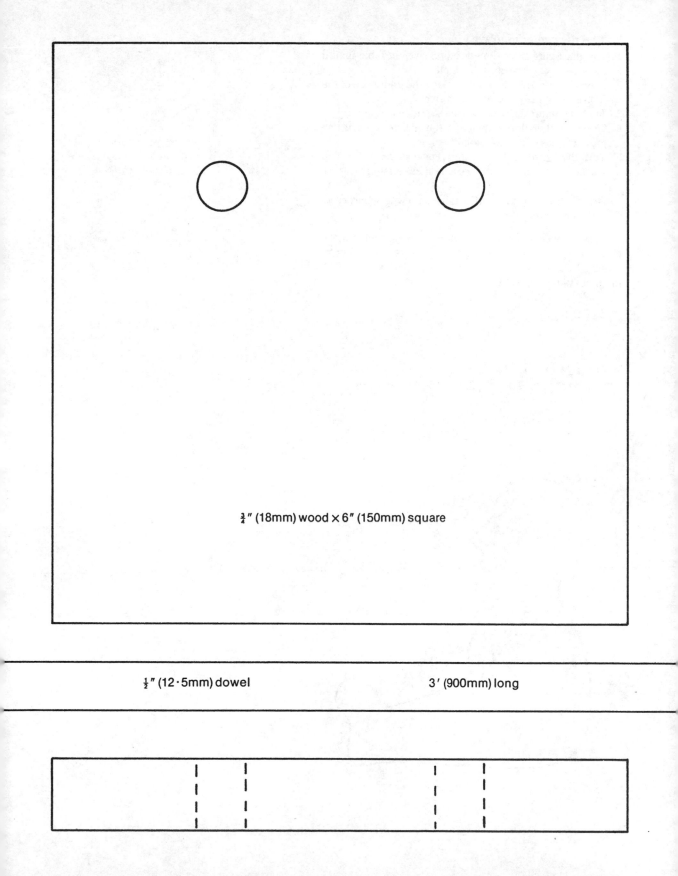

¾″ (18mm) wood × 6″ (150mm) square

½″ (12·5mm) dowel                    3′ (900mm) long

**To find the center of gravity**

1. Lay the figure over the edge of a straight table until it balances, i.e. just begins to topple.
2. Hold it there, and draw a line along the underside of the figure using the table edge as a ruler.
3. Turn the figure 180 degrees and balance it again.
4. Draw another line as before. You will now have two parallel lines quite close together.
5. Turn the figure 90 degrees and repeat stages 1 to 4. You will now have two pairs of parallel lines crossing to form a square.
6. Draw in the diagonals of the square and where they cross is the center of gravity.

To balance the figure so that it comes to rest upright, drill the hole for the balancing bar vertically above the center of gravity: the further away from the center of gravity you drill the hole, the more elliptical the movement.

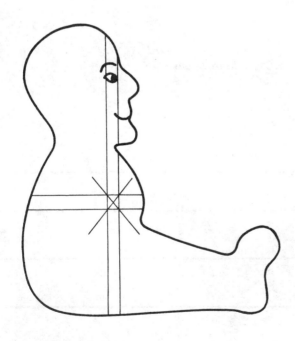

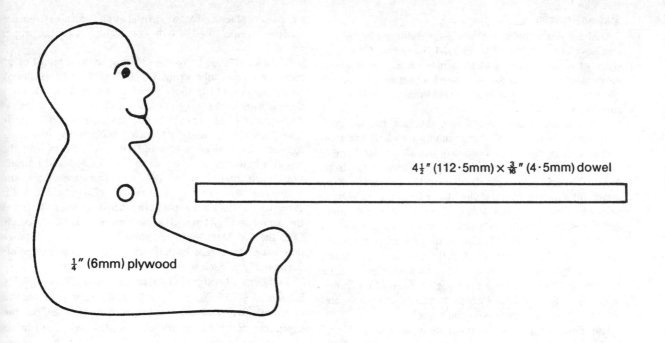

$4\frac{1}{2}''$ (112·5mm) × $\frac{3}{16}''$ (4·5mm) dowel

$\frac{1}{4}''$ (6mm) plywood

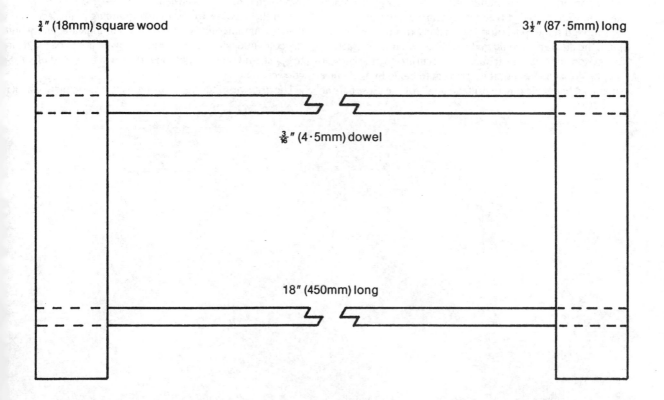

$\frac{3}{4}''$ (18mm) square wood

$3\frac{1}{2}''$ (87·5mm) long

$\frac{3}{16}''$ (4·5mm) dowel

18" (450mm) long

## Tapsalteerie

Tapsalteerie is a toy which will keep children (and adults) endlessly amused. It is of special delight, perhaps, to many types of handicapped children because it can be made to move at a touch, and sometimes needs a gentle nudge, which pleases a child. Its behaviour is so rhythmic that it has a fascinating and soothing effect.

As the name, a good Scots one, suggests, the toy goes topsy-turvy, bottoms up, somersaulting forwards and then backwards, gently down a series of slightly angled parallel bars. The spectator becomes involved as Tapsalteerie drops down from one pair of parallel bars to the pair below, continues his forward somersaults upwards along these bars, reverses at the posts, and does backward somersaults down and across to the opposite posts, where he again goes into reverse and continues this time with forward somersaults, and so on until he comes to a stop at the washers on the last bars. The space left opposite the last bars enables the little man to be lifted out and placed again on top of his frame, where he will go through his performance cheerfully and indefinitely without ever going on strike!

The materials needed are minimal: a piece of $\frac{1}{4}$" (6mm) thick plywood about $4\frac{1}{2}$" (112.5mm) square for the little man; a base of $\frac{3}{4}$" (18mm) wood, $8\frac{1}{2}$" (212.5mm) by $4\frac{1}{2}$" (112.5mm); four posts of $\frac{1}{2}$" (12.5mm) dowel; 10" (250mm) long: fourteen lengths of $\frac{1}{4}$" (6mm) dowel; 4" (100mm) long, and two washers for the ends of the bottom bars. What could be simpler? The base is drilled with four $\frac{1}{2}$" (12.5mm) holes, $\frac{1}{2}$" (12.5mm) away from ends and sides, i.e. $2\frac{1}{2}$" (62.5mm) apart in width and $6\frac{1}{2}$" (162.5mm) apart in length.

Although the explanations for making this toy are rather long, the diagrams should make it all clear. The construction is not too difficult but it must be accurate to the highest degree. To achieve this, it is essential to begin by making a simple jig to enable one to drill the holes for the cross bars at the correct place and at the correct angle, and also to ensure that the bars are glued in to the correct length and the proper angle.

To make the jig, copy the drawing on to a board of $\frac{1}{4}$" (6mm) plywood measuring 12" (300mm) by 5" (125mm) Designate one of the short edges the top and call the edge line o. Draw in the three vertical parallel lines on the left a distances of $\frac{1}{2}$", 1" and $1\frac{1}{2}$" (12.5mm, 25mm and 37.5mm from the side edge, and call them a, b and c. Between a and b top and bottom, draw in horizontal lines 1" (25mm) from the top and bottom edges. Between b and c top and bottom draw horizontal lines $1\frac{1}{2}$" (37.5mm) from the edges, and shade the two rectangular areas off. (This shading is for guidance but does not show in the drawing which illustrates the completed jig.) On both a and b mark points $2\frac{1}{8}$" (53mm from the top. Mark six more points at $\frac{3}{4}$" (18mm) distance downwards from o on both a and b. Join each pair of point horizontally to each other, and to the side edge.

On the right-hand side of the board, draw a line parallel to a, b, and c, $\frac{1}{2}$" (12.5) away from the edge, calling it m. On thi line, mark off similar points to those on the left-hand side bu beginning $2\frac{1}{2}$" (62.5mm) down from the top o, put in si more points $\frac{3}{4}$" (18mm) apart.

These seven points on line m are the center points of the ends of the $\frac{1}{4}$" (6mm) dowel rods. Carefully mark in points $\frac{1}{8}$" (3mm) either side of each of these points.

Similarly find the mid-points on the horizontal lines joining a and b, calling them A, X, B, Y, C, Z and D. Mark in points $\frac{1}{8}$" (3mm) on either side of them.

Join these points to their corresponding points across the board, rounding off the ends. This is to indicate, on the left the holes into which the $\frac{1}{4}$" (6mm) dowels are to be fixed into the post, and on the right, how they will be ended off at the correct angle.

The *drawing* of the jig on the base is now complete, and it i time to put in the strips of wood to make it up.

Begin by making the strip of wood with the rounded edges cut into it, in the following way. Place the drawing over a 12″ (300mm) strip of wood 1″ (25mm) wide and $\frac{1}{2}$″ (12.5mm) thick. Trace on to it the vertical line m, the seven short horizontal lines and the rounded ends of the cross bars. With a $\frac{1}{4}$″ (6mm) bit on their central points, drill out seven holes.

Now saw the strip of wood carefully in half, along the line m. Discard the unmarked piece, and glue the remaining $\frac{1}{2}$″ (12.5mm) width, with the semi-circular holes, firmly to the right-hand side of the board.

On the left-hand side, glue on a 12″ (300mm) strip of $\frac{1}{2}$″ (12.5mm) wood down the side, followed top and bottom by a 1″ (25mm) strip and a $1\frac{1}{2}$″ (37.5mm) strip, side by side as shown on the drawing. You will now have a *raised* bar along each side of your jig, and two shorter *raised* bars top and bottom, on the *left*.

On the left outside strip, mark in the seven center points beginning at $2\frac{1}{8}$″ (53mm) from the top, and calling them, A, X, B, Y, C, Z, and D. (They correspond with A × B etc. already marked on the *drawing*.)

Make a loose bar, for keeping the dowel firmly in place when you are drilling, by cutting a strip of $\frac{1}{2}$″ (12.5mm) wood exactly 9″ (225mm) long but do not glue it in. Mark on it the corresponding points, A, X, etc.

One final addition and your jig will be complete. This addition is to slope the jig in such a way that the drill holes will be at the correct angle.

Prepare a piece of wood 5″ (125mm) long (the width of your board), 1″ (25mm) deep and $\frac{3}{4}$″ (18mm) wide. Taper it off from back to front by about $\frac{1}{8}$″ (3mm) along its length.

To do this, mark in a slope of 5 degrees along each side. Fix the piece of wood in a vice and with a rasp or file scrape in this slope from one side to the other. Glue the shaped surface to the bottom of the board sloping inwards so that the board now slopes downwards from the bottom to the top (see drawing). Now all your drilling should be at the correct angle.

Place a 10″ (250mm) post into the space provided, keeping it firm with the loose 9″ (225mm) bar. Draw a line down the center of the post, and cross it with lines drawn from A to A, B to B, and so on, to give you the center points for drilling. For appearance sake, take your drill only half-way through the posts. You will of course drill two posts only at A, B, C and D, and two others at X, Y and Z!

When you have drilled your four posts, fit in the cross-bars and, removing the spare 9″ (225mm) bar, fit them across the jig into the round spaces you made. Do not glue anything yet, but put the posts with cross-bars into the base and send Tapsalteerie down, making any adjustments necessary.

Make Tapsalteerie according to the diagram. Give him brightly colored clothes and a smiling expression, without too much facial detail — leave that to the children's imagination. Glue a 6″ (150mm) bar of $\frac{1}{4}$″ (6mm) dowel through his hands and set him on top of the frame. He will gently roll over and wend his way, somersaulting downwards, while you and your friends, and all children will lose your heart to him!

When all is well with Tapsalteerie and frame, glue in the bars to the posts, checking all the time that lengths and angles are correct. Glue the posts into the frame, taking care that they match and are upright. Varnish it all and sit back and enjoy your achievement!

A great variety of figures and shapes can be used on the frame as well as Tapsalteerie, such as stars, colored circles, and one, two or three beads on a bar or just a pencil or pen. This gives the toy additional educational value as well as amusement. If children can have access to two versions of this toy, they can have the added fun of races and competitions.

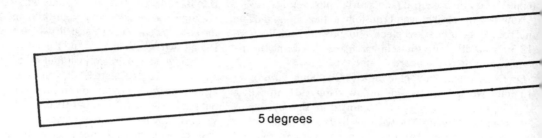

5 degrees

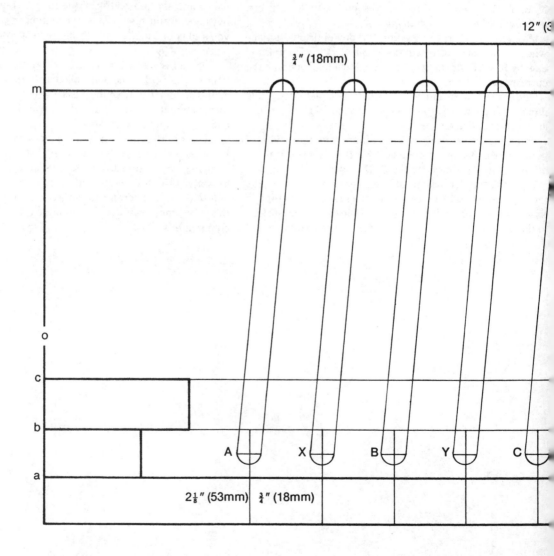

12″ (3

¾″ (18mm)

m

o

c

b

A          X          B          Y          C

a

2⅛″ (53mm)    ¾″ (18mm)

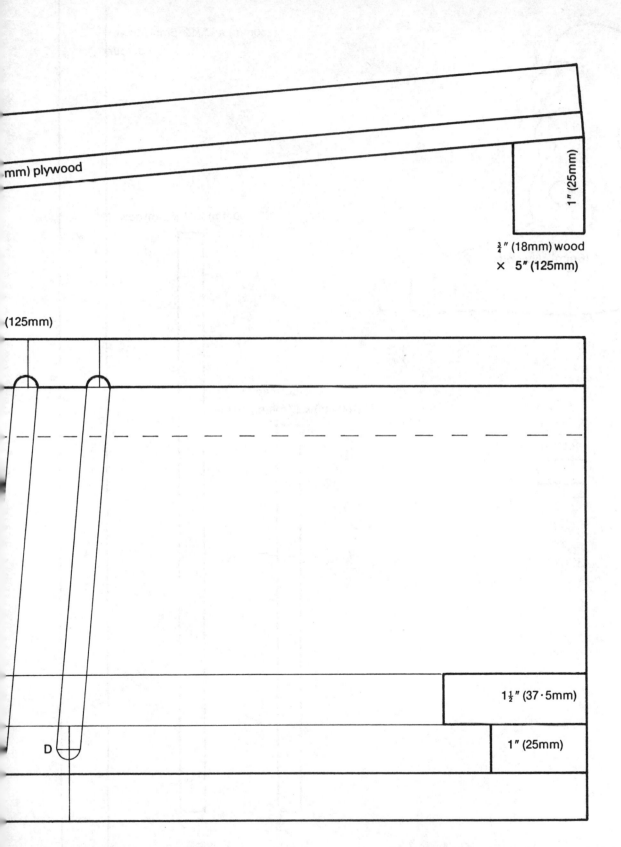

mm) plywood

1 " (25mm)

¾″ (18mm) wood
×   5″ (125mm)

(125mm)

1½″ (37·5mm)

1″ (25mm)

D

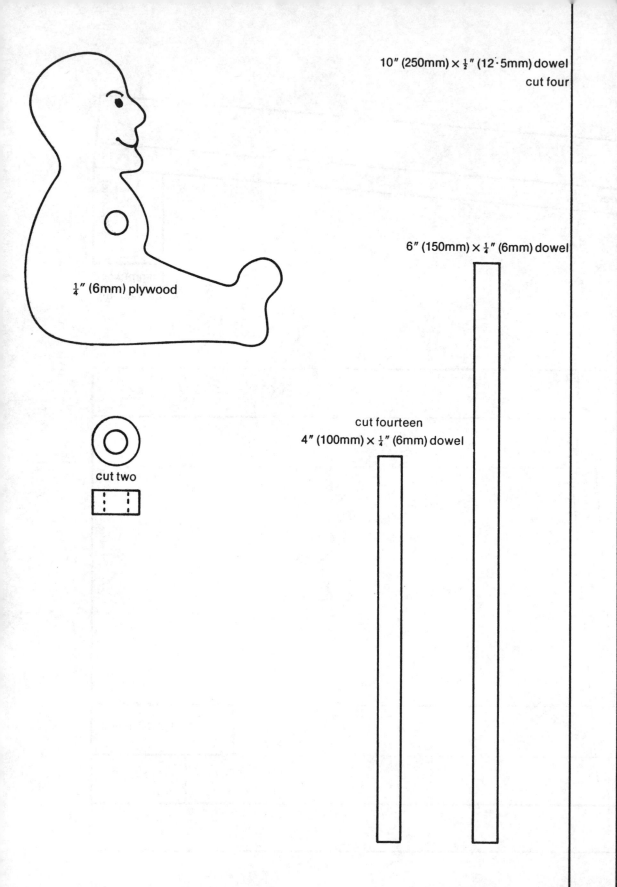

10″ (250mm) × ½″ (12·5mm) dowel
cut four

6″ (150mm) × ¼″ (6mm) dowel

¼″ (6mm) plywood

cut two

cut fourteen
4″ (100mm) × ¼″ (6mm) dowel

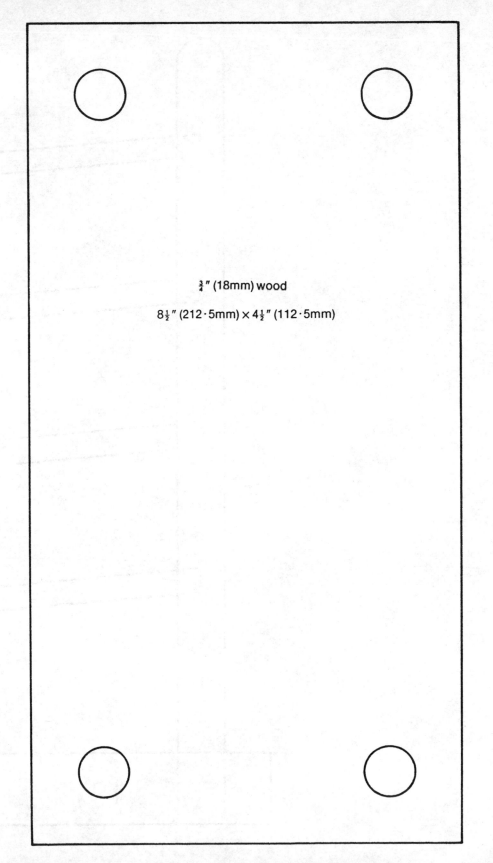

$\frac{3}{4}''$ (18mm) wood

$8\frac{1}{2}''$ (212·5mm) × $4\frac{1}{2}''$ (112·5mm)

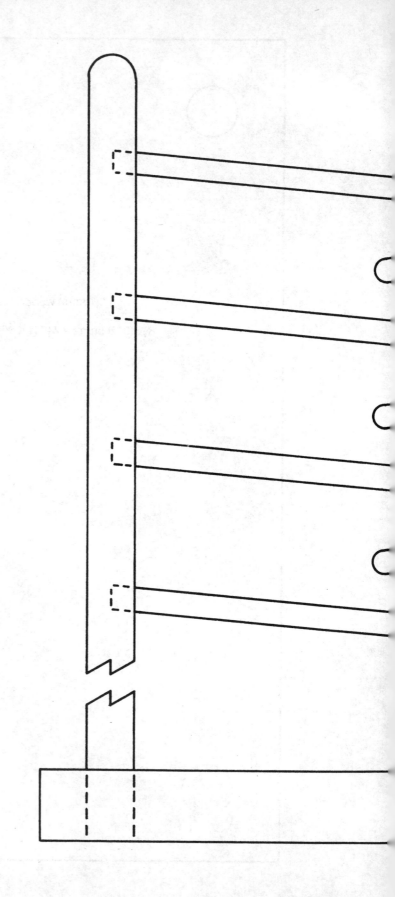

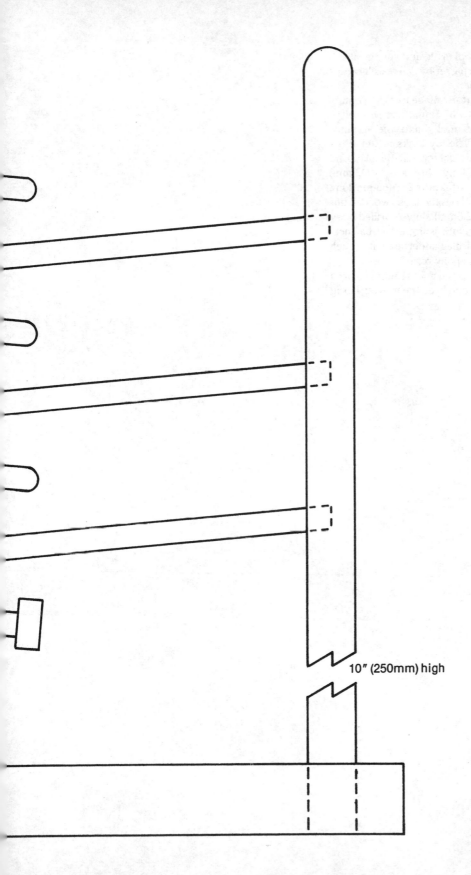

10" (250mm) high

## Jingle Bells

This toy makes a surprising appeal to old and young alike. If it is left out on a table or desk, no passer-by can resist giving it a tap and making the bells jingle!

The measurements for the platform made from $\frac{3}{4}$" (18mm) wood, are $4\frac{1}{4}$" by $3\frac{1}{2}$" (106mm by 87.5mm). The posts of $\frac{1}{2}$" (12.5mm) dowel are placed centrally and the distance between them is $1\frac{3}{4}$" (43mm). The toy looks neater if the holes for the posts are not drilled right through the platform.

The posts are 5" (125mm) long with a $\frac{3}{16}$" (4.5mm) drill hole $\frac{1}{4}$" (6mm) from the top, to take the $2\frac{3}{4}$" (68mm) long metal cross bar. The cross bar carries the loose wooden bar $4\frac{1}{2}$" (112.5mm) long of $\frac{1}{2}$" (12.5mm) dowel drilled very exactly through the center so that it is in perfect balance. This loose bar has a small hole drilled underneath it at each end to carry a bell fixed in with epoxy resin.

On each side of the cross bar, place a $\frac{5}{8}$" (15mm) colored bead to provide a touch of color and keep the moving bar in place.

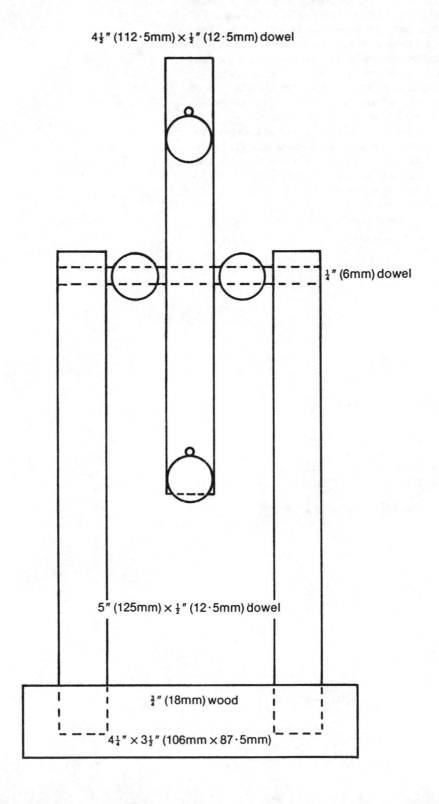

$4\frac{1}{2}''$ (112·5mm) × $\frac{1}{2}''$ (12·5mm) dowel

$\frac{1}{4}''$ (6mm) dowel

$5''$ (125mm) × $\frac{1}{2}''$ (12·5mm) dowel

$\frac{3}{4}''$ (18mm) wood

$4\frac{1}{4}'' \times 3\frac{1}{2}''$ (106mm × 87·5mm)

## The Dwarfs

The dwarfs balance nicely on their little boat and, as their arms are loosely attached with string, they seem to be conversing and gesticulating as they spin up and down and all around. A little bell between them adds to the interest. They balance best if they are made in fairly heavy wood i.e. $\frac{3}{8}''$ (9mm). They are cut out in one piece with their boat and painted in bright colors. The arms are cut in thinner, $\frac{1}{8}''$ (3mm) plywood and attached to the dwarfs with knotted string. Care must be taken that the holes on the posts which carry the central bar are absolutely in line.

The toy is improved if a piece of $\frac{1}{8}''$ (3mm) thick plywood shaped like the hatch, is glued to either side of it. This, with a $\frac{1}{2}''$ (12.5mm) bead on each side of it, gives the exact width, 2$''$ (50mm), required to fill the space between the posts, so that the boat can revolve easily without wobbling. It also provides enough space to drill a hole in the top of the hatch to take a bell, which adds greatly to the charm of the toy.

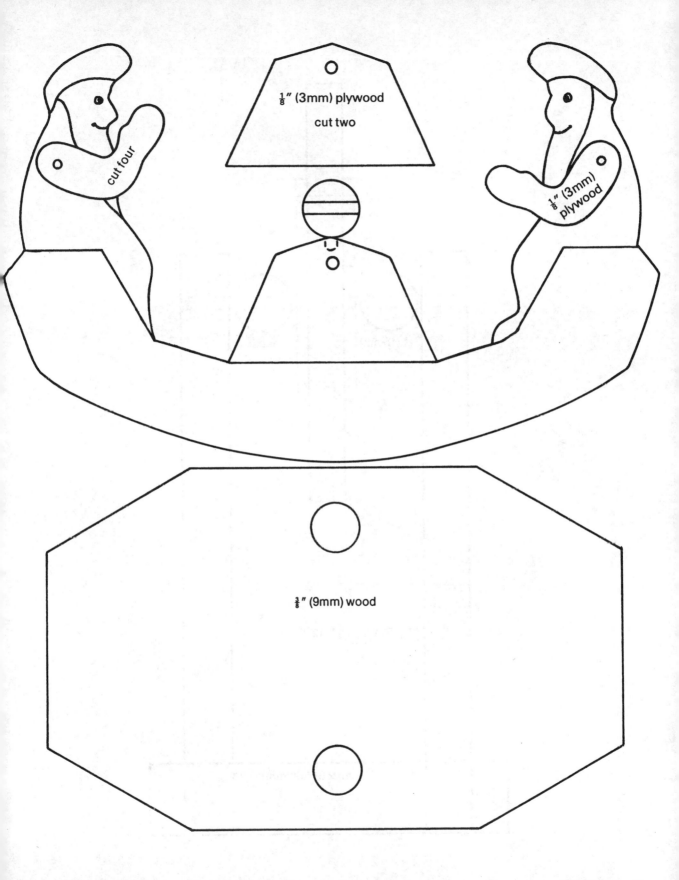

$\frac{1}{8}''$ (3mm) plywood

cut two

cut four

$\frac{1}{8}''$ (3mm) plywood

$\frac{3}{8}''$ (9mm) wood

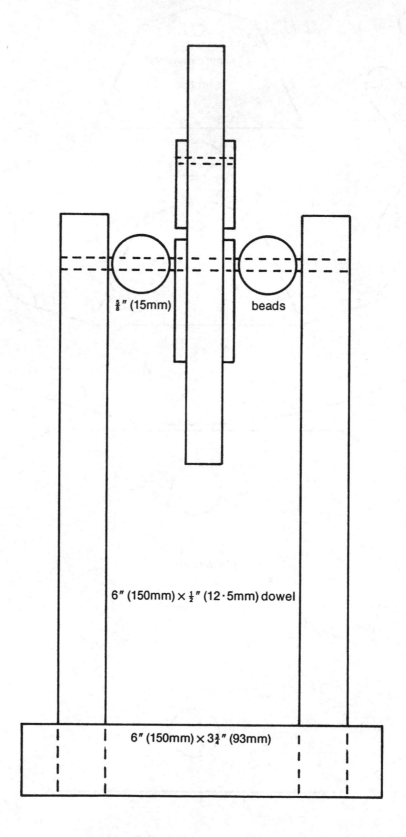

$\frac{5}{8}''$ (15mm)    beads

6" (150mm) × ½" (12·5mm) dowel

6" (150mm) × 3¾" (93mm)

## Blondin

Everybody, young and old, loves Blondin: he exemplifies a principle of balance which is a delight to watch. He can rock from side to side and up and down at unbelievable angles, or he can perch on the extreme edge of his platform, hanging on by one toe-nail so to speak, indefinitely, if so desired.

He is called after the Frenchman who crossed Niagara Falls on a tightrope. This Frenchman also pushed an old lady blindfold in a wheelbarrow on a tight-rope across Niagara Falls — it was, of course, the old lady who was blind-fold! The toy is, I believe, unique because, unlike all the other balancing, counter-weighted figures which are made in wood or in metal with two legs fixed as one, Blondin's legs are jointed at the hips, and he can balance on one at a time. A young boy, who was playing with him, discovered this, because he moved a leg which had been rather loosely riveted, and the toy was still in balance. We were both of us surprised and delighted to find out how much more exciting and unusual Blondin's performance was in consequence.

The toy is not at all difficult to make and requires very little in the way of materials. For the stand, make a circular platform of $\frac{1}{4}$″ (6mm) wood, 3″ (75mm) in diameter, drilled centrally to take a $\frac{1}{2}$″ (12.5mm) dowel about 10″ (250mm) high, to allow him free movement. The dowel is fixed into a base made of $\frac{1}{2}$″ (12.5mm) or $\frac{3}{4}$″ (18mm) wood, which can be a 3″ (75mm) to 5″ (125mm) circle, square or hexagon as desired; the base also is drilled centrally. A piece of $\frac{1}{4}$″ (6mm) ply, 4″ (100mm) by 5″ (125mm) is sufficient to make Blondin.

Begin by making the stand, then drill and cut out Blondin in $\frac{1}{4}$″ (6mm) plywood. Paint and varnish the separate parts, giving him a cheerful expression but without too much detail. Rivet the arms very tightly to the body so that they cannot be moved, and rivet the legs less tightly so that one leg can move and not the other (this is not difficult).

Blondin will work either with his arms straight in front of him or with them in a lower position. He looks more impressive with his arms outstretched, but is a little more difficult to balance in that position. You must decide before you rivet the arms which position he is to adopt.

It is a good idea to prepare the cane in advance. If it is rather dry and brittle, soak it in water for an hour or so. Wipe off the superfluous water with a cloth and, for Blondin, cut off a 27″ (675mm) long piece of $\frac{3}{16}$″ (4.5mm) cane. Bend it gently into a rounded arch at the center. Mark the center point, and points $\frac{1}{2}$″ (12.5mm) on each side of the center. This will show you where to place the hands, with a wooden washer between. Round off the arch with your hands from the center downwards, gradually bringing the ends of the cane nearer to each other.

When you consider you have achieved a satisfactory shape, either place the ends evenly in a wide, deep vase, or in two holes drilled 9″ (225mm) apart in a block of wood. Leave the arch to take on its shape until you are ready to use it.

Now take the cane and slip Blondin on to it with a wooden washer between his hands until the midpoint on the cane is inside the washer. Work some glue along the cane between the hands and washer. Keep the center of the arch held out in front of him with the ends of the cane sloping slightly backwards. Lay him down on his hands in this position, supporting his legs from underneath until the glue is set. This joint at the hands must be fixed immovable because the balance of the toy depends on it.

When the glue is set, make marks 9″, 10″, 11″ and 12″ (225mm, 250mm, 275mm and 300mm) from the outside of the hands, along the cane on each side. Slip three 1″ (25mm) colored beads on to the cane at each end between these marks. Do not glue them on — keep them from slipping off by twisting a rubber band on to the ends of the cane.

Set Blondin on his feet on the stand. He may skate and slither about a little at first, but you must gently stroke the cane near the center of the arch until he is in balance. If he leans forward too much, stroke the cane gently backwards from the arms downwards, and vice versa.

Do not despair if you think he will never balance! He will! He must! You can see from the photographs that he does: it is only a question of coaxing him into position and it does not take long.

You may find it easier to get the balance if you have the cane a little longer and the beads correspondingly lower, but I find that I can get a satisfactory balance with the measurements just given, and the toy does not take up too much space. Once you have got Blondin to balance, glue the beads into the position located on the cane, and on to each other, and when they are set, cut off the surplus cane.

Sometimes, even if you have your two sides exactly matching, and your beads the same weight, Blondin will incline (annoyingly) more to one side than to the other. This means that there is something wrong with the arch and it has to be corrected there. If he leans to the left, slightly raise the arch on the left, close to the hands, by gently stroking the cane upwards and outwards, and vice versa.

The balance is most subtle and must be found by a certain amount of trial and error, but, once established, it should not vary. Sometimes, with a change of temperature, the cane spreads out too much from the bottom, but this can be compensated for by pulling the ends of the cane together by means of a rubber band above the beads, and leaving them like that for an hour or so or overnight.

Blondin can balance on a cork in a bottle. He can turn on a small coin and perform very agile gymnastic feats on one leg or on two. With reasonable treatment he very rarely falls off his platform, but even if he does he comes to no harm. Children soon learn to handle him carefully enough to make the most of his really sensational possibilities. He is an extremely popular toy.

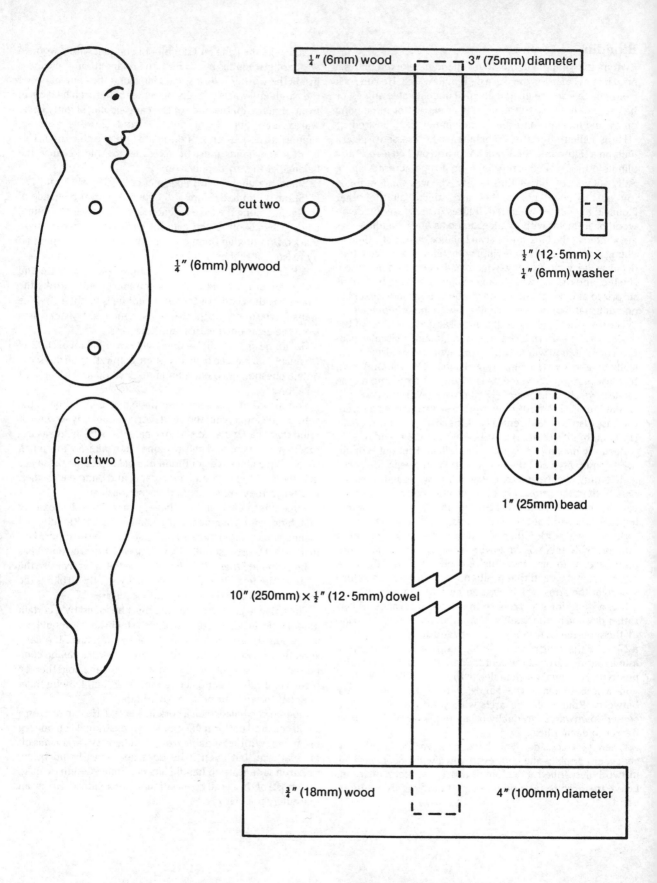

¼″ (6mm) wood          3″ (75mm) diameter

cut two

¼″ (6mm) plywood

½″ (12·5mm) ×
¼″ (6mm) washer

cut two

1″ (25mm) bead

10″ (250mm) × ½″ (12·5mm) dowel

¾″ (18mm) wood          4″ (100mm) diameter

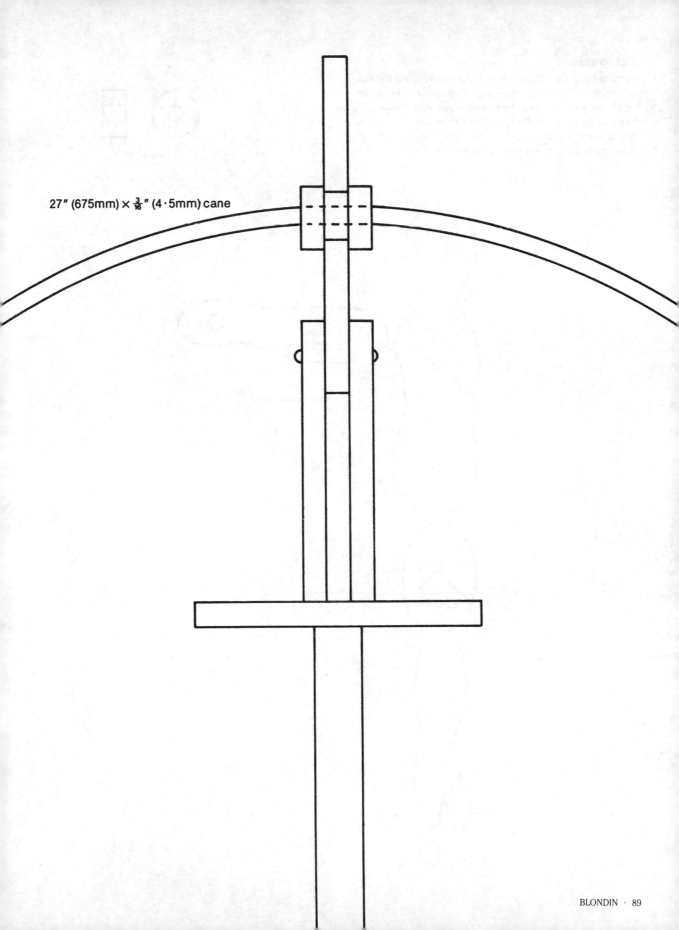

27″ (675mm) × $\frac{3}{16}$″ (4·5mm) cane

## Petronella

Petronella has the same potential as Blondin, but she is a real ballerina and performs in a most spirited way. I designed her after my young friend had shown me that Blondin could balance on one leg. The length of cane and the number of beads and the construction is the same as for Blondin. She is a dainty little lass and has a charm all her own.

washer

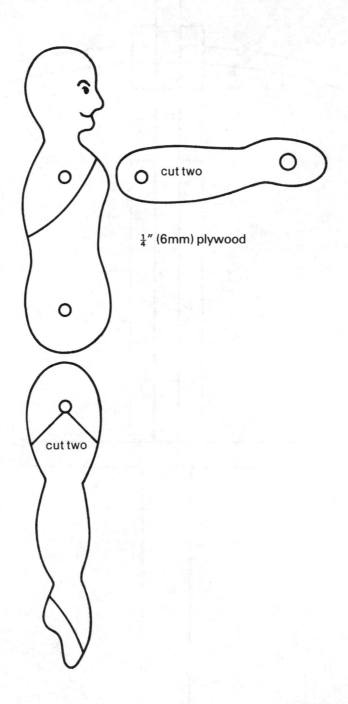

cut two

¼" (6mm) plywood

cut two

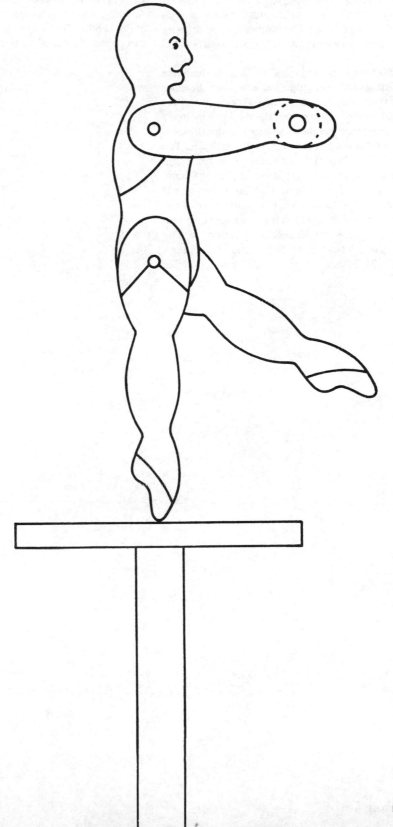

## Pegasus

Pegasus is another original toy and gives a most fascinating performance, plunging and rearing as he cavorts around his stand. He does not have wings like his prototype but he does give the appearance of being a flying horse. The drawing was made for me by a Swiss artist friend, Monsieur Wüst of Morges.

I find it best to paint the body and the legs of the horse separately before gluing them together, when dry. In order to get the animal into the correct position, I lay the parts over a drawing of the horse before gluing them on one by one.

Pegasus requires more weight to balance him than Blondin does and I use five beads instead of three on each side. The first bead will be 9″ (225mm) from the saddle, so the length of cane on each side will be 14″ (350mm) plus $\frac{1}{4}$″ (6mm) through the saddle, i.e. $28\frac{1}{4}$″ (706mm) in total. However, it is best to start with a 30″ (749mm) length of cane, marking the center at 15″ (375mm) and proceeding to balance Pegasus in exactly the same way as for Blondin and Petronella. The frame requires a larger base, 5″ (125mm), and a longer post, 11″ (275mm) to 12″ (300mm) than for Blondin or Petronella.

## Little Peg

It may amuse some readers to make Little Peg, who is a half-sized version of Pegasus, so the drawings are included here. Actually, his performance is not quite so sensational as that of Big Brother (he's only a baby after all), but he is easier to carry around or send by post.

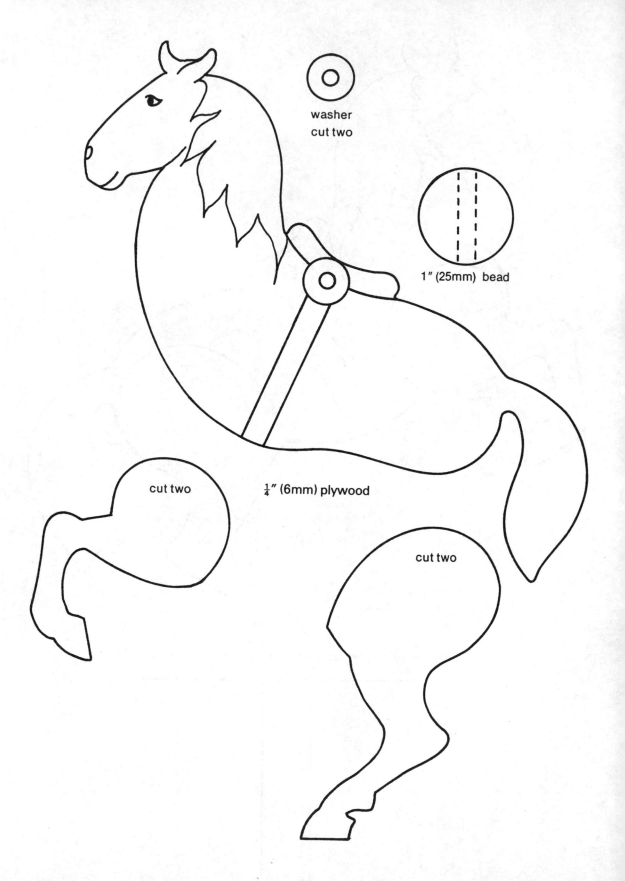

washer
cut two

1" (25mm) bead

cut two

¼" (6mm) plywood

cut two

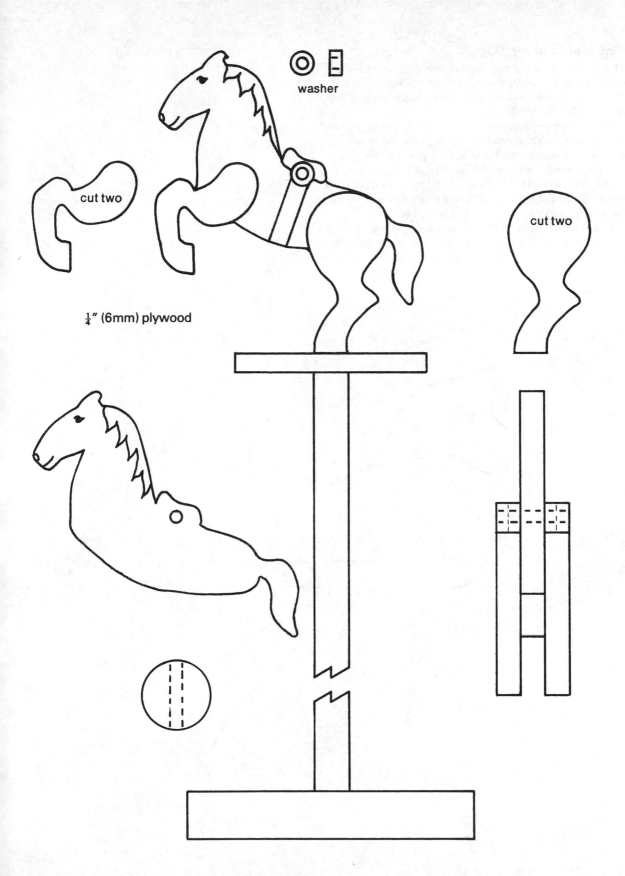

washer

cut two

cut two

$\frac{1}{4}''$ (6mm) plywood

## One Man and his Dog

This toy is very simple to make and does not really need any explanation as the drawings show clearly what has to be done. It illustrates balance by a single weight, even though the man has two beads!

The counter-weight to keep the man in an upright position has to curve forward under him, and for the dog in running position, it has to be out backwards. If you want the dog to beg, the weight has to be immediately underneath him.

The rivets should not be fixed too tightly, so that the arms and weights can be put into different positions which adds to the interest and educational value of the toy.

If the weights are correctly adjusted, the figures will always return to the upright position however much they get pushed around. A valuable example perhaps!

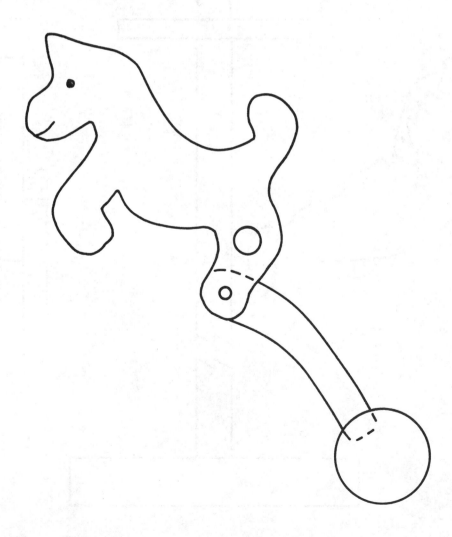

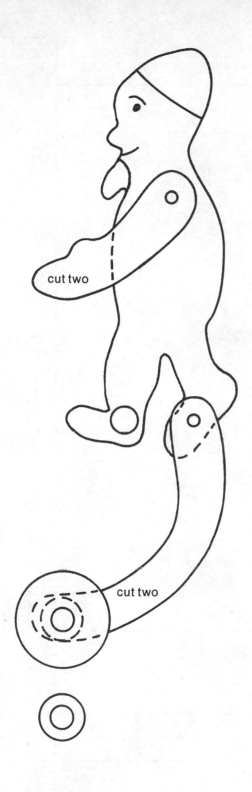

cut two

cut two

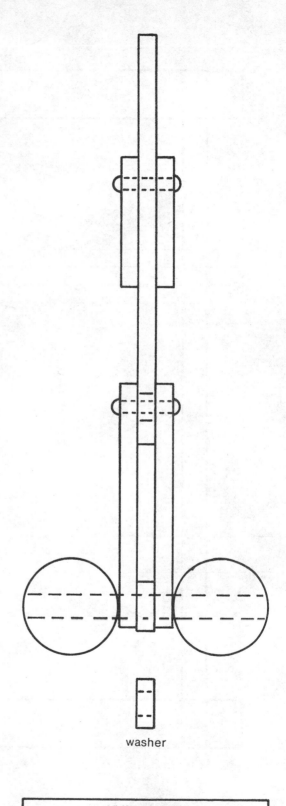

washer

¼" (6mm) dowel

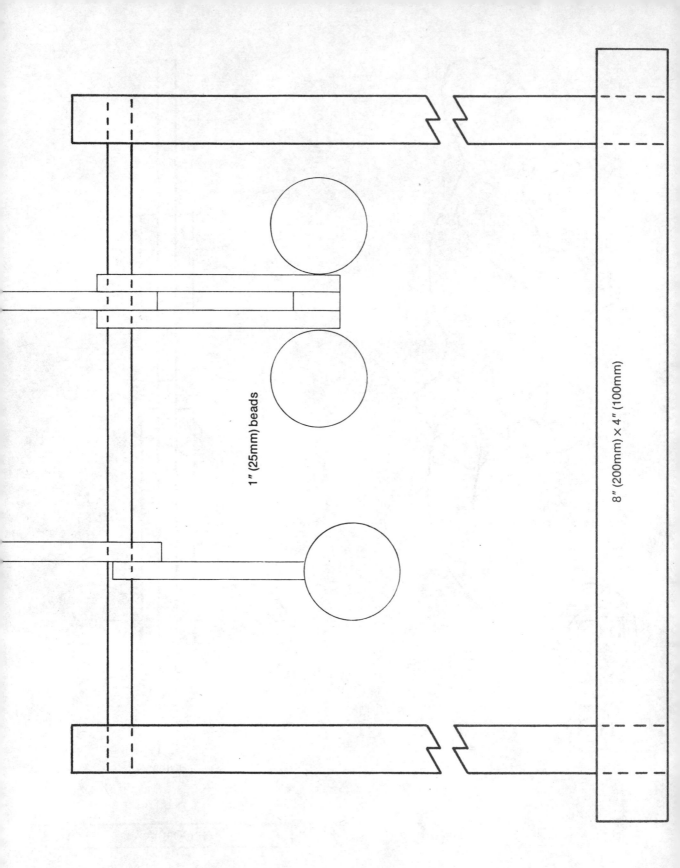

1" (25mm) beads

8" (200mm) × 4" (100mm)

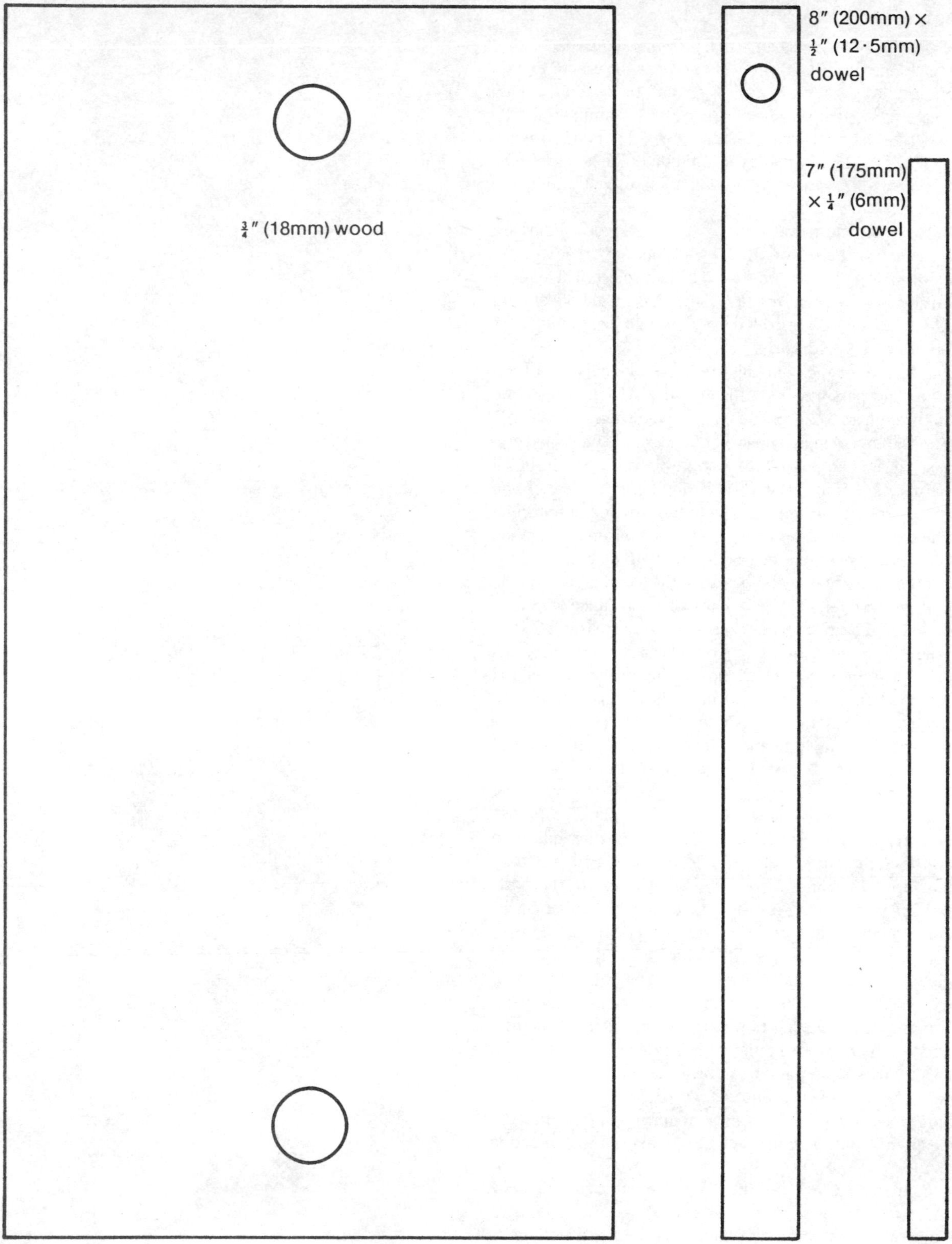

$\frac{3}{4}''$ (18mm) wood

8" (200mm) ×
$\frac{1}{2}''$ (12·5mm)
dowel

7" (175mm)
× $\frac{1}{4}''$ (6mm)
dowel

## Jack and Jill

Jack and Jill (who can go up a hill) counterbalance each other on each end of a short frame. The frame consists of two 6″ (150mm) long metal bars $\frac{1}{8}$″ (3mm) thick, which pass through a $\frac{1}{2}$″ (12.5mm) thick dowel, 8″ (200mm) long. The dowel is drilled with two $\frac{1}{8}$″ (3mm) holes, $2\frac{1}{4}$″ (56mm) apart, i.e. $1\frac{1}{8}$″ (28mm) each side of the mid-point. The holes must be exactly in line with each other and straight through the dowel.

In two 3″ (75mm) pieces of $\frac{1}{2}$″ (12.5mm) wood, holes are drilled the exact size and the same distance apart as those in the dowel, but they are not taken right through. The ends of each steel bar are inserted into these. A central hole at right angles to these holes is drilled right through these end-pieces to support Jack and Jill.

The figures of Jack and Jill are made by doubling a pipe-cleaner and passing it first through a $\frac{3}{4}$″ (18mm) bead and then through a 1″ (25mm) bead, and gluing it in, splaying out the ends to make legs. The larger bead should be drilled previously at right angles to take a single pipe-cleaner through it for arms. Glue it in place. Double another pipe-cleaner and push it through the central hole in the wooden endpiece of frame from the under side and into the bottom of the bead where the legs come out; glue it in at both places.

Put the figure at one end on top of the wooden bar and the one at the other end below it. They should balance perfectly. You will find that the balance is delicate and easily affected by slightly moving the figures or their arms or legs. A bell hooked over one arm of each figure adds to the interest, but slows down their progress and alters the balance somewhat.

Their stand is made from two lengths of 1″ (25mm) square wood 18″ (450mm) long and four posts of the same wood 7″ (175mm) high, to be fixed on each end, and backed by a piece of wood or plywood, $\frac{1}{4}$″ (6mm) thick, 6″ (150mm) long and $2\frac{1}{2}$″ (62.5mm) wide, to keep it all in place. Two 18″ (450mm) lengths of $\frac{1}{2}$″ (12.5mm) dowel are also required to go through the posts, which should be drilled with a slightly larger drill, 1″ (25mm) from the top. The top of the posts should be bevelled off, for the sake of appearance, and a $\frac{1}{4}$″ (6mm) hole drilled centrally $\frac{1}{2}$″ (12.5mm) deep in the top of each one to carry a colored 1″ (25mm) bead on a small piece of dowel. The stand looks even nicer if the posts at one end are made 1″ higher (25mm) than those at the other end, but this necessitates drilling the holes in them at an angle of 5 degrees, which is more difficult. It is perfectly easy to slope the stand by slipping in a book or a piece of wood about 1″ (25mm) high under one end.

Small flags of your choice or country inserted into the beads, with split cane as flag-poles, make a most effective finish.

In point of fact, Jack and Jill can revolve quite satisfactorily along two lengths of dowel placed 5″ to 6″ (125mm to 150mm) apart, between two chairs, but the stand adds enormously to the quality of the toy.

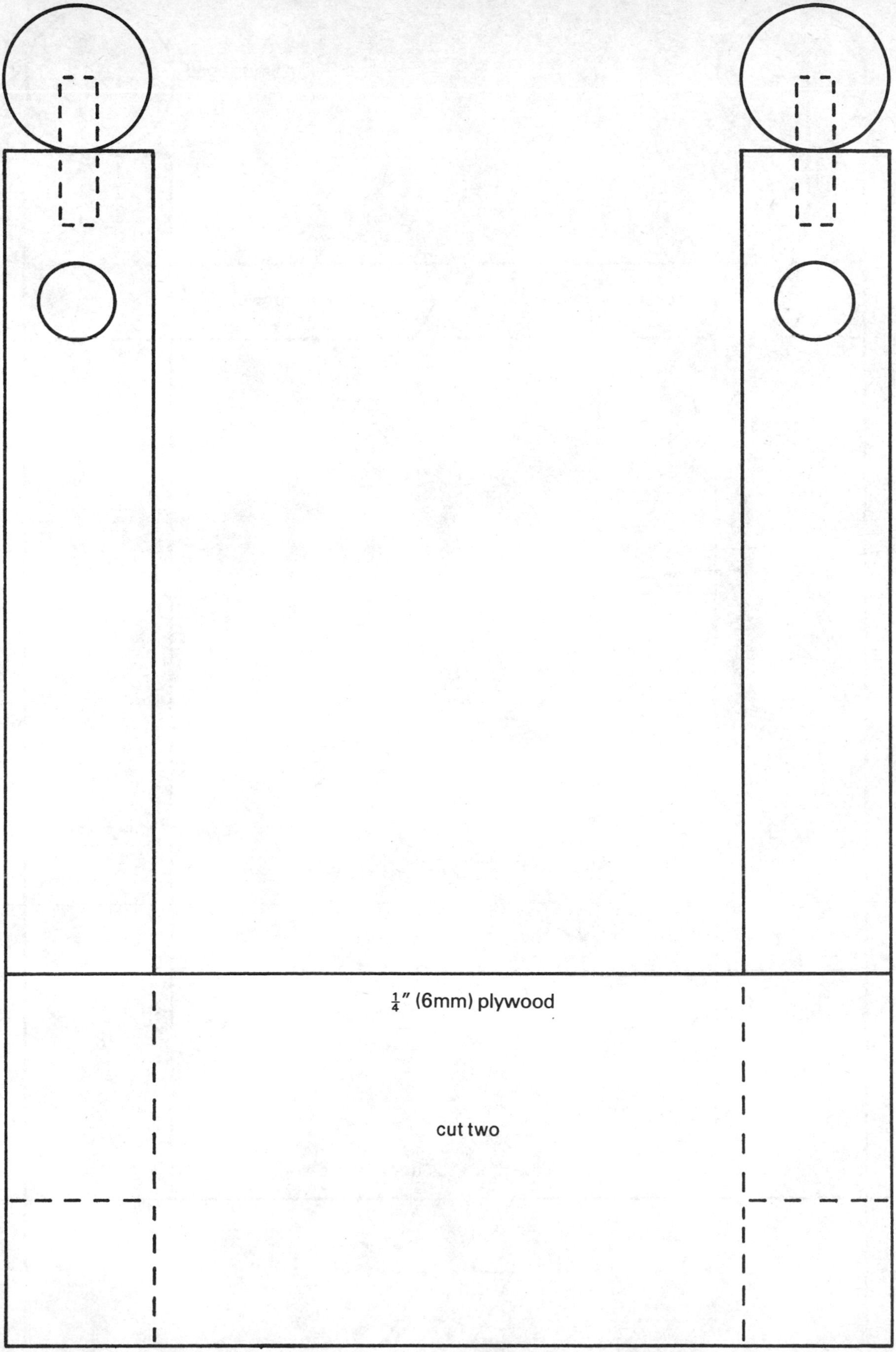

$\frac{1}{4}''$ (6mm) plywood

cut two

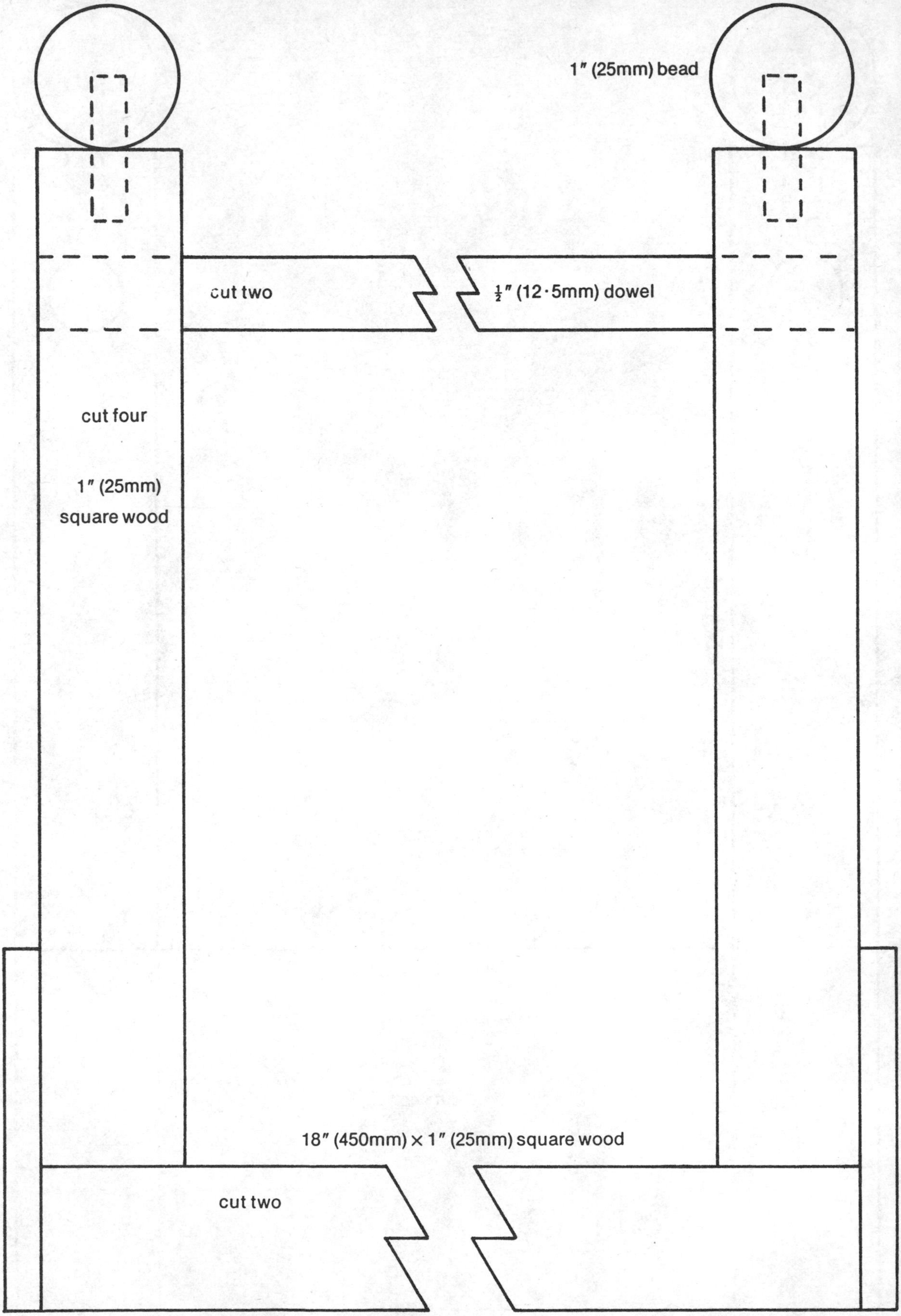

1″ (25mm) bead

cut two

½″ (12·5mm) dowel

cut four

1″ (25mm)
square wood

18″ (450mm) × 1″ (25mm) square wood

cut two

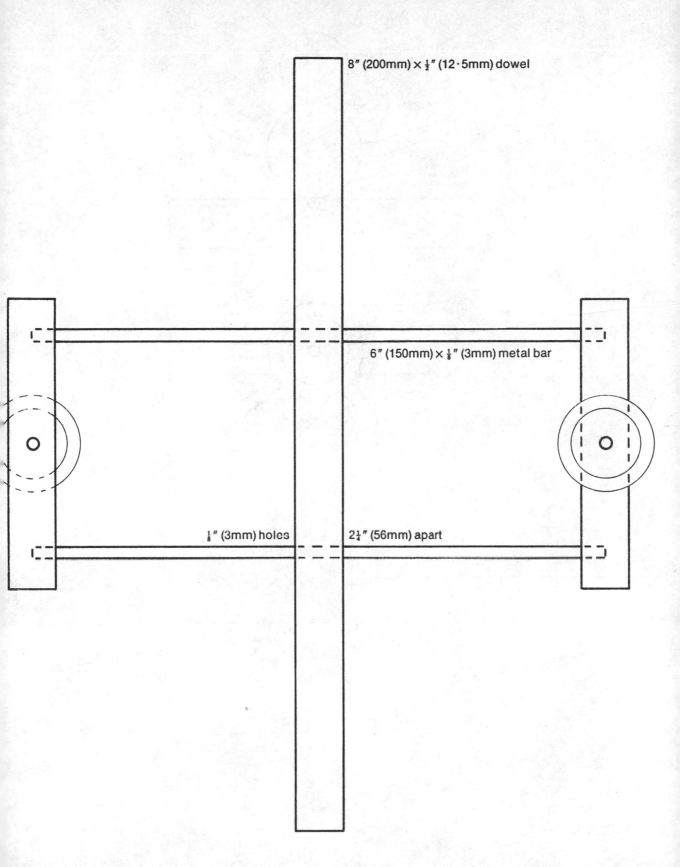

8" (200mm) × ½" (12·5mm) dowel

6" (150mm) × ⅛" (3mm) metal bar

⅛" (3mm) holes    2¼" (56mm) apart

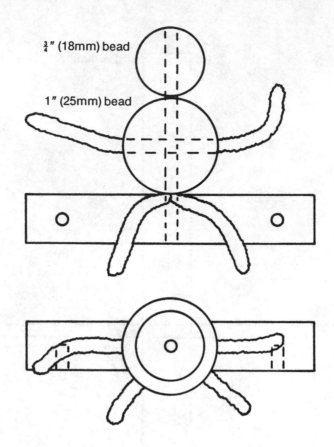

¾" (18mm) bead

1" (25mm) bead

## The Climber

The Climber is an easy, rewarding toy to make. It is a never-ending joy to small children. In its simplest form it can take a basic human shape with arms stretched upwards, or it can be a little girl, a sailor, or a bear as you choose. The essential point is to drill a hole at an angle through the hands to enable a string to pass loosely through them. The upper ends of the strings are passed through holes drilled in either end of a bar above, and secured with a knot. The bar can move freely as it is suspended by a loop of string, secured through another hole drilled through the mid-point of the dowel. The other ends of the string finish some 3 or 4 feet (900–1200mm) further on with a bead at the end.

The toy is manipulated by pulling first on one string and then on the other, so that the figure climbs zig-zag to the top, and falls straight down again when pressure is released. The drawings (taken from *Wooden Toys that Work*) show very clearly how it is made and how it works.

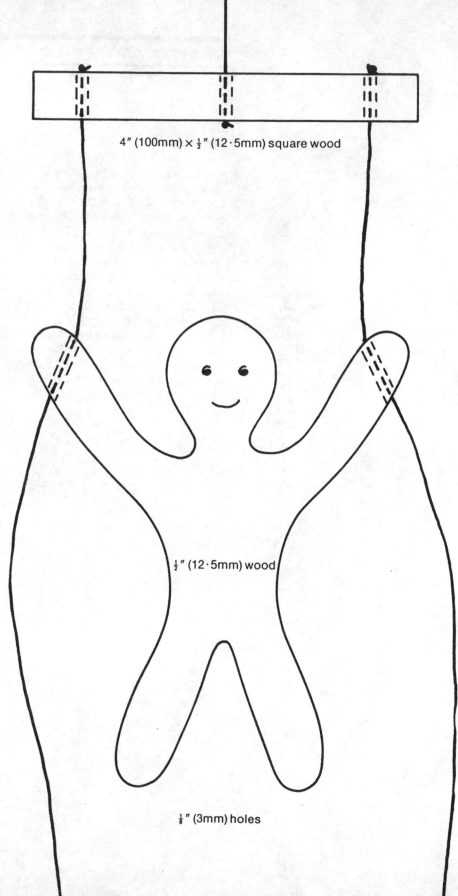

4″ (100mm) × ½″ (12·5mm) square wood

½″ (12·5mm) wood

⅛″ (3mm) holes

## The Magic Waterfall

This fascinating toy of Eastern origin and sometimes known as a Jacob's Ladder, consists of six or more pieces of wood of identical size, held together by three tapes, one central at one end, and two either side of center at the other end. A convenient size is $\frac{1}{8}''$ (3mm) thick plywood, measuring $3\frac{1}{4}''$ by $2\frac{1}{4}''$ (81mm by 56mm) and fifteen pieces of ribbon or colored tape, $4\frac{3}{4}''$ (106mm) long. If you are making colored waterfalls, which are more interesting than plain ones, color your strips of wood before you cut them to size.

The tapes are glued to the underside of one piece of wood, pass between it and the next piece, and are attached to it on the upper side at the corresponding opposite end (1). Begin by attaching $\frac{1}{2}''$ (12.5mm) of tape to the end of one piece of wood (A) in the center, and $\frac{1}{2}''$ (12.5mm) of two tapes to the other end in such a way that there is clear passage for the central tape when the pieces of wood are joined up (2a). Now place A face downwards with the attached ribbons underneath (2b), bring them up from underneath and lay them along the wood (2c).

Put tapes on a second piece of wood (B) and place it exactly above A, leaving its attached ribbons spread out (underside downwards) (3).

Now attach the single tape, which has come from the top end (t) of the lower side of A, to the bottom end (b) of the second piece of wood B, on the upper side, and similarly attach the two tapes from the bottom end (b) of the lower side of A to the top end (t) of B on upper side (3).

The ribbons must be attached so that each piece of wood can lie exactly above the other, neither too tight nor too slack. For clarity in drawing 3, more space is shown between the pieces of wood than the ribbons would allow. Continue in the same way, putting tapes on C, laying it above B and joining B's tapes to C and so on until all six pieces of wood are joined together, noting that the last piece of wood does not carry tapes of its own.

If the pieces of wood are painted, say, red on one side and blue on the other, then tapes will be attached to three pieces of red wood and to two of blue or vice versa. If red is face down to start with and blue is the side up, then the next piece of wood must be placed blue side down and red side up, and so on, like facing like. This will ensure, surprisingly enough, that the toy will end up all blue on one side and all red on the other when it is spread out.

To manipulate: when all the pieces of wood are joined together, arrange them in a pile, with the pieces of wood on which only the $\frac{1}{2}$ inches (12.5mm) of tape show at the top and bottom. Pick the toy up by the top piece, letting the other pieces fall downwards. Press the top piece gently downwards, forwards and then backwards, or vice versa, so that the tapes change over and each piece of wood seems to fall from the top to the bottom in turn. It is an illusion of course but a very convincing one.

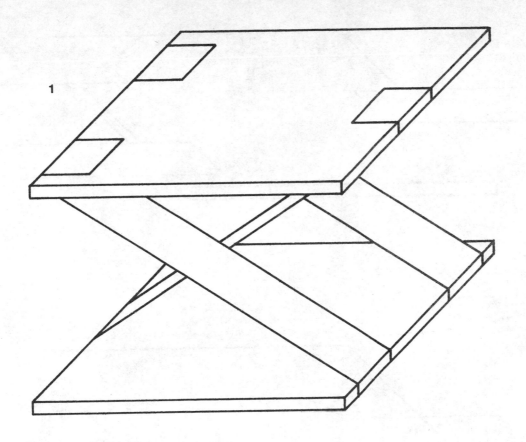

**1**

| ½″ (12·5mm) tape | 4¾″ (118mm) long | cut fifteen |

⅛″ (3mm) plywood

3¼″ (81mm) × 2¼″ (56mm)

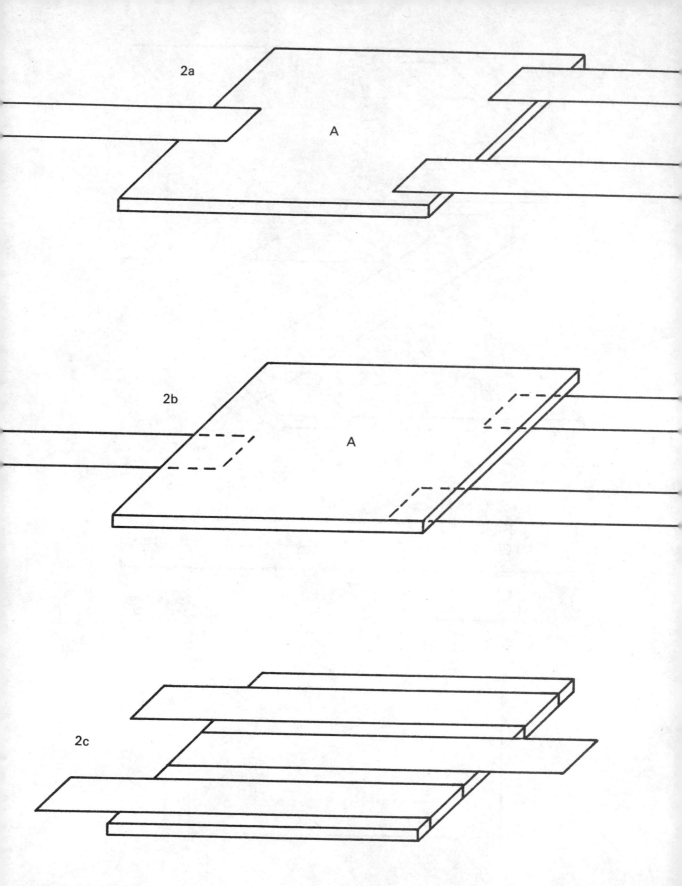

2a

A

2b

A

2c

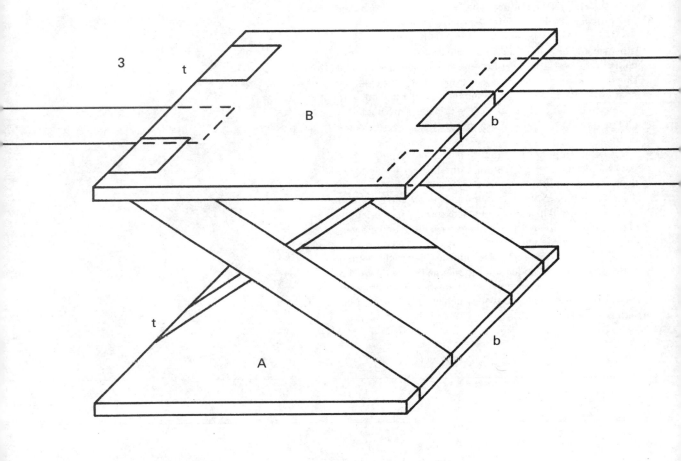

3

t

B

b

t

A

b

## Ziggedy Man

The success of this toy depends on making the board for the little man absolutely accurately. The peg-holes must be the same distance apart on both sides and in line, and come exactly half-way between each other across the board. If you copy the drawing carefully, you should have no trouble.

The board should be of $\frac{1}{2}''$ (12.5mm) wood — good plywood is best — 2' (600mm) long and 4" (100mm) wide. Draw lines parallel to the sides $\frac{3}{4}''$ (18mm) from each side and $2\frac{1}{2}''$ (62.5mm) apart. Lay your copy of the drawing exactly over the board; mark off nine points on each side along the parallel lines. The bottom holes are opposite each other and $\frac{3}{4}''$ (18mm) from the bottom. The holes on one side (say the left) proceed at $2\frac{3}{4}''$ (68mm) intervals. On the other side, the first hole above the bottom one is $1\frac{3}{8}''$ (34mm) away, and the other seven holes at $2\frac{3}{4}''$ (68mm) from each other. You can of course reverse the order of the pegs from left side to right side. Checking, by compass if you like, that your eighteen points are exactly where they should be, drill them out with $\frac{1}{4}''$ (6mm) drill. It looks neater if the drill holes are not taken all the way through the board, but they must be the same depth.

Cut eighteen pegs of $\frac{1}{4}''$ (6mm) dowel 1" (25mm) long — they should stand up $\frac{3}{4}''$ (18mm) from the board — and glue them into the holes.

Copy the little man in $\frac{3}{8}''$ (9mm) plywood and send him down the board. The critical points for success are the length of the arms and the underarm measurement. Paint and varnish him as your fancy chooses.

A bar about 1" (25mm) thick should be glued to the bottom of the board on the under side, so that he comes down at a slight angle. Children of course find it hilarious if he jumps off his board or turns upside down, which he may well do if his path is too steep.

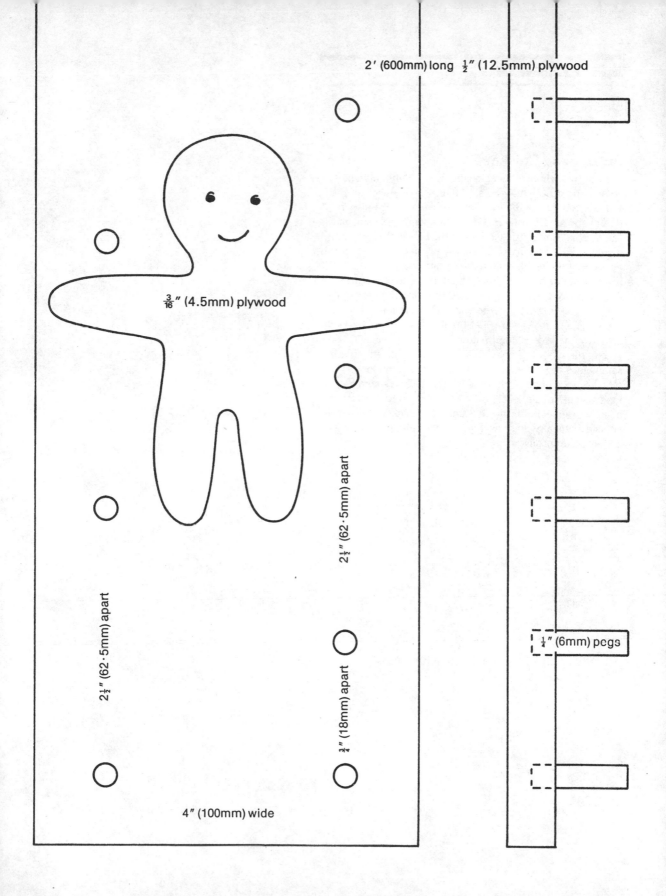

2′ (600mm) long  ½″ (12.5mm) plywood

3/16″ (4.5mm) plywood

2½″ (62·5mm) apart

2½″ (62·5mm) apart

¾″ (18mm) apart

¼″ (6mm) pcgs

4″ (100mm) wide

## Push-Along Chicken

Cut out two whole chicken shapes in $\frac{1}{4}$" (6mm) plywood as shown and drill them with a $\frac{1}{4}$" (6mm) hole where marked. Cut one top-half shape for the middle of the bird also in $\frac{1}{4}$" (6mm) plywood, finishing at the dotted semi-circle and glue it to one side. Cut out the shape for the four legs in $\frac{1}{8}$" (3mm) plywood i.e. thinner wood to allow for movement. You will notice that the feet lie along the circumference of a circle. It is advisable to draw in this circumference before cutting to make sure of getting the feet exactly along the line. Drill a $\frac{5}{16}$" (7.5mm) hole in the center of the circle. Paint and varnish the parts and make sure that the leg piece revolves easily around a piece of $\frac{1}{4}$" (6mm) dowel.

Glue the parts together, fixing the legs in position with a small piece of $\frac{1}{4}$" (6mm) dowel about $\frac{5}{8}$" (15mm) long.

Make a $\frac{3}{8}$" (9mm) drill hole in the chicken's shoulder to take a length of dowel about 18" (450mm) long, with a large bead at the end for propulsion. The chicken makes an amusing squeaky noise as it gets pushed along, and his foot action is humorous.

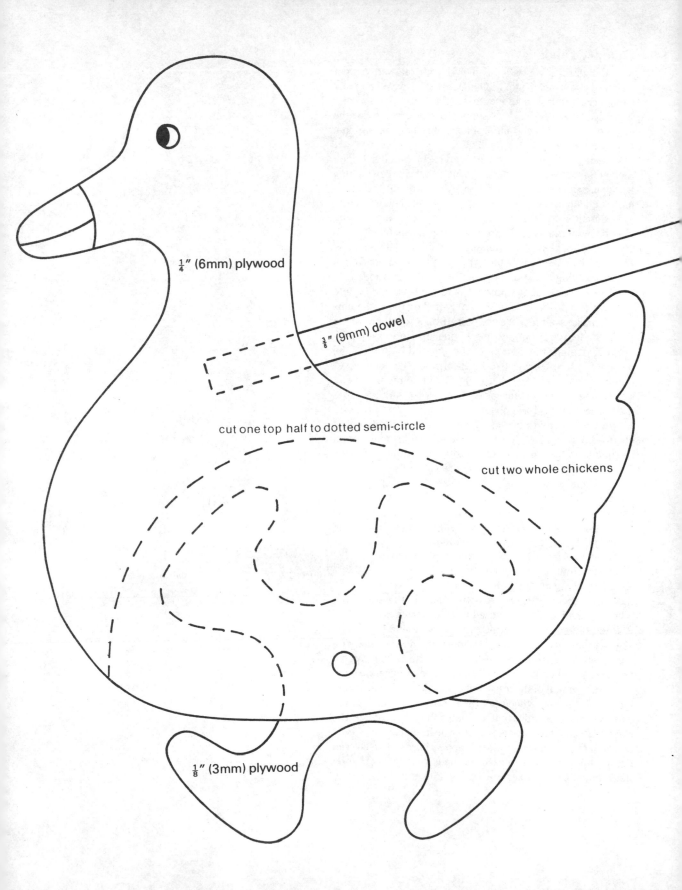

¼" (6mm) plywood

⅜" (9mm) dowel

cut one top half to dotted semi-circle

cut two whole chickens

⅛" (3mm) plywood

# Dumpty Duck

This delightful toy was available as a kit ready to be put together a few years ago. I call it Dumpty Duck. When I first came across it, it was love at first sight! Easily put together from the drawings, it is very simple to make, except for the egg which presents certain problems, but these are fascinating to overcome.

At the age of about eleven or twelve, children in a Rudolf Steiner School are introduced to Woodwork, first by making wooden eggs by hand, and then by attempting the much more difficult task of making wooden spoons. This particular egg is created from a piece of wood 2" by 2" and 3" long (50mm by 50mm and 75mm long). All that is needed is a clamp, a rasp, plenty of sandpaper and lots of patience. The egg can, of course, easily be turned in a lathe but it is much more satisfying to make it by more primitive methods.

There must be many approaches to the task, and I quote my own as a possible help. I begin by finding the mid-points of all four sides of the piece of wood and marking them with a small St George's cross in ink — pencil is too easily obliterated. Around the centers of the top and bottom of the block of wood, I draw two concentric circles, one of 1" (25mm) radius and the other of $\frac{1}{2}$" (12.5mm) radius. Then I sketch an egg on the four faces of the wood. All these lines are my landmarks throughout.

Now I am ready to begin, placing the wood firmly in the clamp, and rasping off in turn all the four sharp edges, from the middle of the egg towards the top and bottom, removing the 'shoulders' between the eggs drawn on the four faces. The wood must be moved continuously in the clamp, round and round, as one tries to achieve an egg-shape, imagining strongly the egg lying hidden in the block of wood, feeling where there are bumps which need smoothing, admiring the grain and so on, and gradually rounding off one end flatter and the other more pointed as the work develops.

Another little help is to cut two pieces of tape, one $6\frac{1}{2}$" (162.5mm) long and the other $8\frac{1}{4}$" (206mm) — these are the measurements of the egg crosswise and lengthwise around when finished, and can be used to gauge progress.

When the egg is finally the proper shape and beautifully smooth, place it upright in the hollow of the duck's back. You will surely feel extremely satisfied and proud as you watch it bounce up and down as the duck is pulled or pushed along!

The movement of the toy depends on the egg being in contact with all four wheels as they move, so the egg and carriage must be adjusted to each other to produce the rolling effect. No two eggs will ever be identical!

A very fine version of this toy is appearing as a hen with an egg revolving on her back. It is made by toymaker John Buckland at Clive, near Shrewsbury, England.

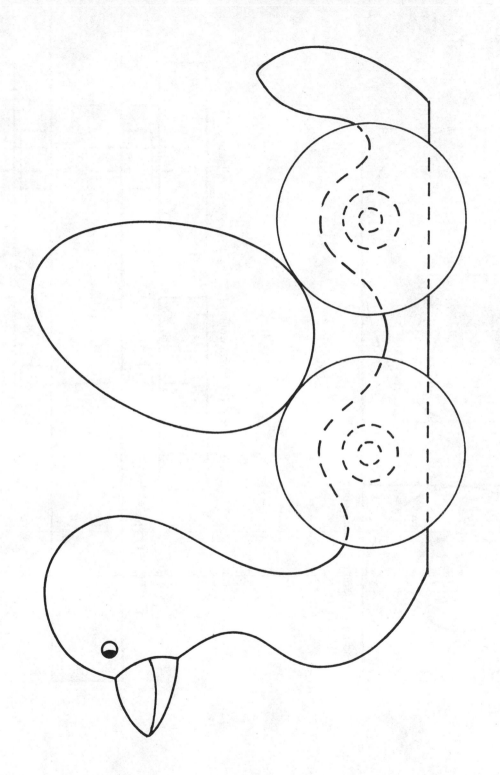

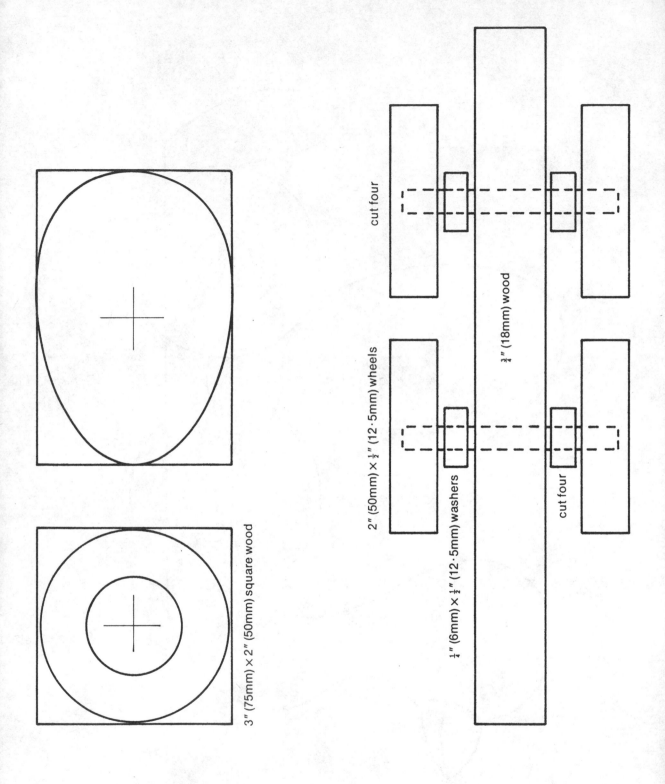

3″ (75mm) × 2″ (50mm) square wood

cut four

$\frac{3}{4}$″ (18mm) wood

2″ (50mm) × $\frac{1}{2}$″ (12·5mm) wheels

$\frac{1}{4}$″ (6mm) × $\frac{1}{2}$″ (12·5mm) washers

cut four

## Skippy

The idea for this delightful toy was given to me by a Danish friend who had made up a prototype from memory of a toy he had much enjoyed as a child. In his original, a long-legged boy, by means of a wire through the arms, makes a little girl, indicated by a cloth skirt and long hair of wool, skip and turn somersaults.

His version is not quite suitable for a book, and I pass on the idea in the form of rather robot-like characters, though it could assume other forms. This one was devised by Michael Hanson and works very well. It is quite simple to make but requires very accurate drilling.

To avoid disappointment, if you have not had much experience of drilling holes deep into rather narrow dowel, do begin by practising on odd lengths. Mark the central point at each end of a short length of $\frac{3}{8}''$ (9mm) dowel, and fix it firmly, absolutely upright, in a clamp. With an awl or bradawl make a small hole in the center, and enlarge it with a counter-sink bit. With a narrow bit, say $\frac{3}{32}''$ (2mm), and with your *hand*-drill upright, drill a hole through the dowel centrally a short way. Then turn the dowel upside down and repeat your actions from the other end, and so on until both bore holes meet. When you can do this successfully, continue with larger bits until you have enlarged the hole to the size you need.

Do not be discouraged if your bit goes off the straight or comes through the side at first; with practice you will master this quite difficult task and go on to succeed in driving bigger drill-holes to the depth you want. Always begin with a small bit, in a *hand*-drill, and make sure your wood is at right angles to the clamp.

Once you have established a straight channel, say $\frac{1}{4}''$ (6mm), through a piece of wood with a hand-drill, you can proceed to greater widths with an electric drill, preferably fixed in a drill stand.

I find it very helpful in moving from a smaller bit to a larger one, to work a counter-sink-bit around the hole several times, to save damage to the edges which a larger bit easily inflicts.

For the bodies we have used two pieces of $1\frac{1}{2}''$ (37.5mm) diameter, cylindrical wood $1\frac{3}{4}''$ (43mm) and $1\frac{1}{2}''$ (37.5mm) long respectively. The legs, arms and necks are made of $\frac{3}{8}''$ (9mm) dowel, the heads of $1''$ (25mm) plain wooden beads, and the skipping rope from about $16''$ (400mm) of $\frac{1}{8}''$ (3mm) galvanised (aluminium) wire which is easy to bend but stays firm. The arms are made of $\frac{3}{8}''$ (9mm) dowel drilled centrally to take the wire. The legs of the taller figure are $2\frac{3}{4}''$ (68mm) long. They are glued into holes drilled in a wooden platform made of $\frac{1}{2}''$ (12.5mm) wood and measuring about $7\frac{1}{2}''$ (187.5mm) by $4''$ (100mm). The platform requires to be solid to keep the toy firm when in action. The legs of the smaller Skippy are $2''$ (50mm) long; a $\frac{1}{4}''$ (6mm) length of each is glued into the body. Taper the legs slightly for the sake of appearance.

Having made and painted your Skippies, glue in the arms, legs, necks and heads, and secure the legs of the bigger one into the platform. Then take about $18''$ (450mm) of $\frac{1}{8}''$ (3mm) wire and make a loop of about $9''$ (225mm) at one end, by bending it round the neck of a 1 lb jam jar and straightening it off at right angles to go through the $2\frac{1}{2}''$ (62.5mm) long arms of the smaller, mobile Skippy. Bend it up at right angles for $\frac{3}{4}''$ (18mm) and bend it again at right angles to go through the arms of the other Skippy: finishing it off into a handle. Slip on a $1''$ (25mm) length of $\frac{3}{8}''$ (9mm) dowel drilled centrally to give it a grip; $\frac{3}{4}''$ (18mm) dowel as illustrated is equally good.

The skipper should be able to touch the ground from time to time, and the wire can easily be adjusted between the figures to produce that effect.

When you get this toy working, I think you and all the family will want to play with it for hours on end!

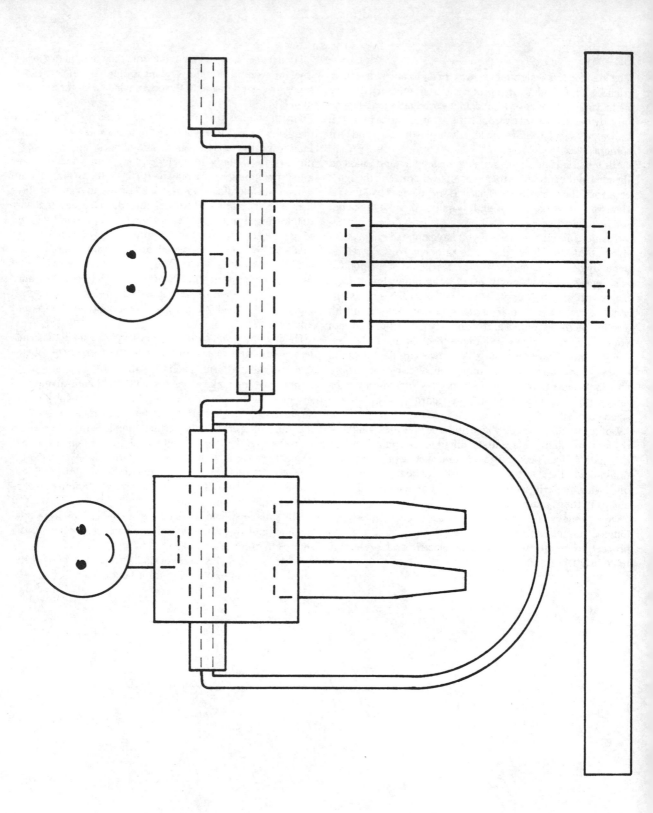

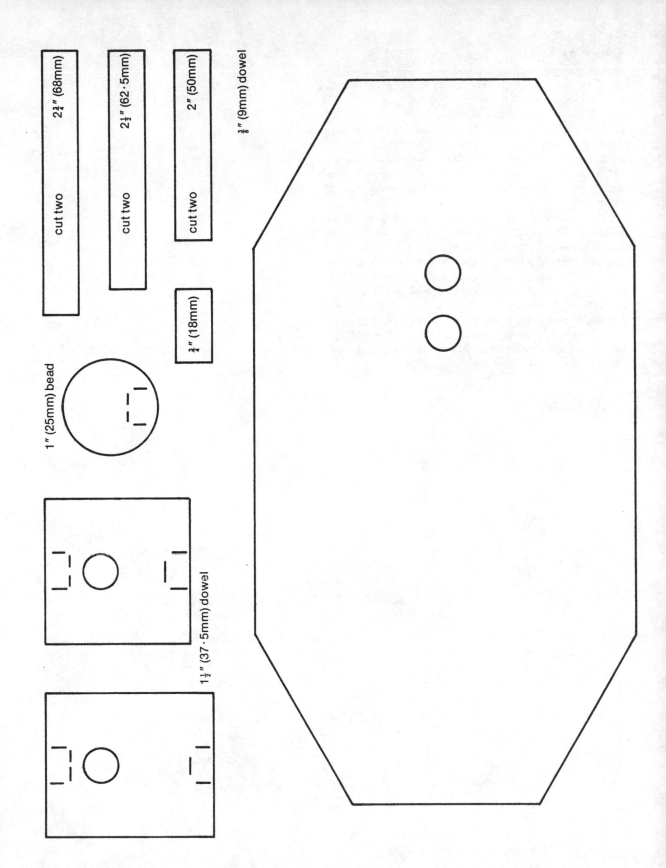

2¾″ (68mm)

cut two

2½″ (62·5mm)

cut two

2″ (50mm)

cut two

⅜″ (9mm) dowel

¾″ (18mm)

1″ (25mm) bead

1½″ (37·5mm) dowel

## Two-Way Tops

Why is a simple spinning top so fascinating? I really do not know the answer but did you know that tops are equally simple and fascinating to make?

Draw on to $\frac{3}{16}$" (4.5mm) plywood circles of either $1\frac{1}{2}$" (37.5mm), $1\frac{3}{4}$" (43mm) or 2" (50mm) diameter. Drill through the centers with a $\frac{1}{4}$" (6mm) bit and saw out the circles. Smooth them and paint them, and insert in each one a short, $1\frac{1}{2}$" to 2" (37.5mm to 50mm) length of $\frac{1}{4}$" (6mm) dowel, slightly rounded at each end by two or three turns of a pencil sharpener.

If the top is in balance it will spin silently either way up. When balance is established, glue it together and you can have endless fun with this most simple of toys, especially if you have painted patterns so that the colors will blend effectively, lemon and prussian giving green, crimson and blue making purple and so on. Dots will appear as a ring.

If difficulty is found in cutting circles, use a hexagon or a hexagram shape. Do you remember that the radius of a circle goes exactly six times round the circumference? Join each consecutive point and you get a hexagon, and every second one and you get its star, a hexagram.

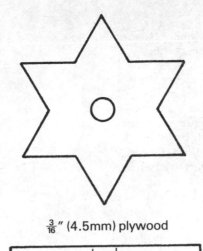

$\frac{3}{16}''$ (4.5mm) plywood

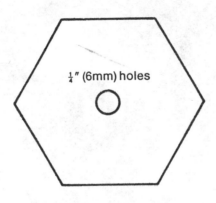

$\frac{1}{4}''$ (6mm) holes

$\frac{1}{4}''$ (6mm) dowel

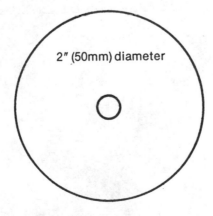

2" (50mm) diameter

## The Gymnast

When I first made this toy and called it the Gymnast, I had no idea that this word meant 'naked' in Greek, nor that gymnastic exercises were performed in the nude in the days of Ancient Greece. However, a coat of paint makes him look brighter and possibly more respectable to modern mankind!

The toy is a development of the well-known Monkey-on-a-Stick and is a good, solid toy for small children to experiment with. I use a similar figure to the Acrobat but in heavier wood, $\frac{1}{4}''$ (6mm) plywood, with only one hole in the hands to attach him to his post, and one hole in his feet to attach him to his stick. The diagrams show exactly how he is made. Use string for the joints and attachments to posts to obtain flexibility.

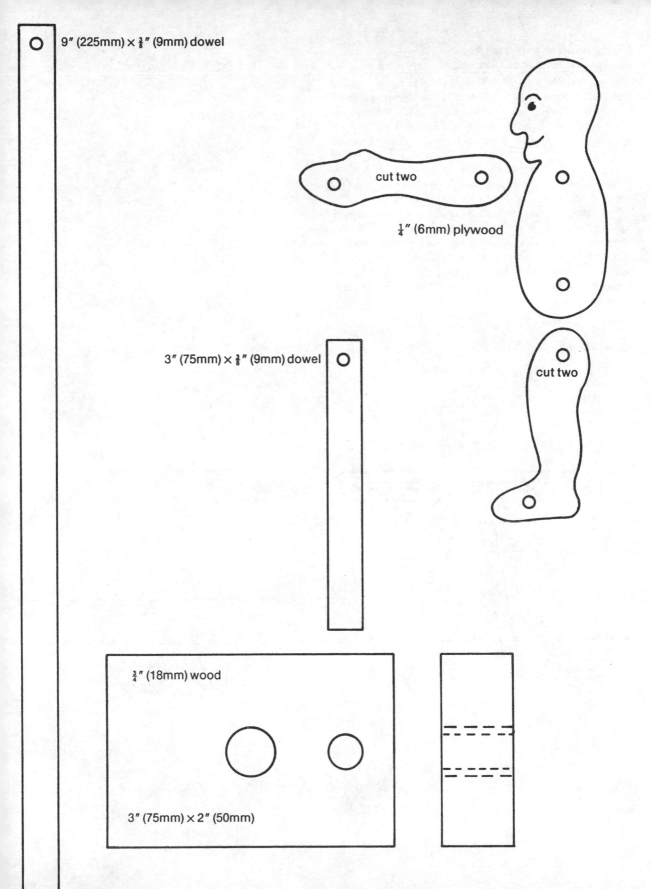

9" (225mm) × ⅜" (9mm) dowel

cut two

¼" (6mm) plywood

3" (75mm) × ⅜" (9mm) dowel

cut two

¾" (18mm) wood

3" (75mm) × 2" (50mm)

## Dolls from Pipe Cleaners

Bend a pipe cleaner (white for preference) in half; push the bent portion into a $\frac{3}{4}''$ (18mm) plain wood bead for the head and glue it there. Bend up the ends of another pipe-cleaner so that they meet in the middle, and thread it through the first one at right angles to it, below the head, leaving about $\frac{1}{4}''$ (6mm) for the neck. Bind each leg and arm with wool, leaving a little space at the end of the arms for hands (which children enjoy hooking on wherever possible) and pad the body out with wool. Two dots for eyes are quite sufficient for the face, and hair of colored wool can be glued on.

The dolls can be dressed as boys or girls and whole families can quickly be created in this way out of scraps of material. These dolls fit nicely into the Cradle for which directions are given, or will sit on chairs or stools. While it is much quicker and easier to sew these dolls into their clothes, it should be remembered that children much prefer to be able to dress and undress them.

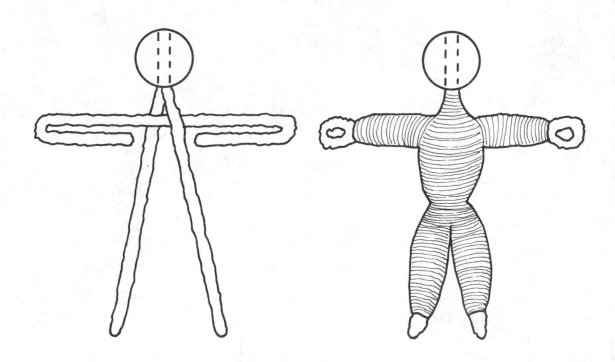

# INDEX